A
TEA WITCH'S
CRYSTAL BREWS

A TEA WITCH'S CRYSTAL BREWS

Empowering the Magick of Tea
with Crystal Grids

S. M. HARLOW

WEISER BOOKS

This edition first published in 2025 by Weiser Books, an imprint of
Red Wheel/Weiser, LLC
With offices at:
65 Parker Street, Suite 7
Newburyport, MA 01950
www.redwheelweiser.com

Library of Congress Cataloging-in-Publication Data available upon request.

Cover and interior design by Sky Peck Design
Crystal illustrations copyright © AlenaZenArt and Bloomella
via Creative Market

Typeset in Footlight
Printed in China
WMP
10   9   8   7   6   5   4   3   2   1

For Zander

Contents

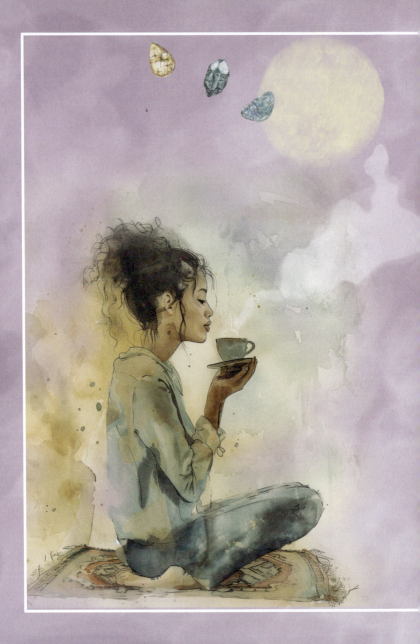

Introduction

ear friends, I humbly thank you for stepping onto this path with me and exploring the beautiful power of tea magick. Writing my first book, *A Tea Witch's Grimoire: Magickal Recipes for Your Tea Time,* was a labor of love, a journey that allowed me to immerse myself in my passion and craft. It was also the perfect way to honor those who took the time to raise me, teach me, believe in me. These precious souls will never be forgotten, for I hope their wisdom has been made eternal through my words.

Since creating the grimoire, I have continued to grow and expand my craft. I found great inspiration and power through the experiences shared with friends and loved ones. Their presence brought new light to my practice, illuminating the profound connections we forge with each other and the world around us. It was in these moments of shared energy and intention that I stumbled upon a revelation—the captivating synergy between tea and crystal grids.

In the exploration and intertwining of these two ancient practices I discovered a potent magickal experience. The energies that flow between tea and crystals are profound, creating a harmonious dance of intention and manifestation. This revelation opened a new chapter in my journey, one that I am eager to share with you in this book, where the art of tea-making converges with the mystical power of crystal grids, unleashing a transformative force that transcends the ordinary and unlocks the extraordinary within.

The allure of tea magick and crystal grids has always been their ancient, mystical nature, which invites us to embrace and explore their greater power and possibilities. Tea, with its rich history and cultural significance, has long been revered for its ability to nourish both body and soul. It serves as a conduit for intention, a vessel through which we can infuse our daily rituals with mindfulness and purpose. Similarly, crystal grids, steeped in the wisdom of sacred geometry and the metaphysical properties of gemstones, offer a captivating approach to intention setting and energy alignment.

As we dive into the world of tea magick, we are drawn to the enchanting properties of various teas and herbs, each with its own energetic signature and potential for transformation. Whether it's the soothing embrace of chamomile, the invigorating energy of green tea, or the comforting warmth of spiced blends, teas hold the power to elevate our consciousness and deepen our spiritual connections.

Likewise, the allure of crystal grids lies in the intricate weaving of energy that unfolds as we arrange carefully selected gemstones in sacred patterns. These crystalline formations act as conduits, amplifying our intentions and creating a harmonious flow of energy that resonates with our deepest desires.

It is within the interplay of these ancient practices that we find a connection unlike any other. The magickal marriage of tea magick and crystal grids unveils a world where intention and energy converge, where the subtle alchemy of herbs and the radiant energy of crystals intertwine to create a potent magickal experience.

The transformative power of combining tea magick and crystal grids is a revelation that transcends the boundaries of conventional spiritual practices. Individually, both tea magick and crystal grids still hold profound potential for transformation, yet when united, their synergy becomes an extraordinary force for change and manifestation.

Together, they invite us to explore the depths of our intentions, to align our energies with the natural world, and to manifest our aspirations with unwavering clarity. The transformative power of this union is a testament to the ancient wisdom that guides us, offering a path to inner alchemy and external manifestation unlike any other.

My intention for this book is to unveil the captivating synergy between the art of tea-making and the mystical power of crystal grids, offering readers a transformative journey into the realm of ancient wisdom and magickal practices. I aim to empower individuals to infuse their daily lives with intention, mindfulness, and spiritual connection.

This book explores the individual intricacies of tea magick and crystal grids. What you will find offered here:

- ❖ The art of intentional tea preparation, and guidance in selecting teas that resonate with your goals and aspirations.
- ❖ A primer on the mesmerizing world of crystals—how to choose them for their energetic qualities, how they pair with tea blends, and how to design grids that will empower you to align your intentions and amplify the energetic fields of both tea and crystal.
- ❖ Daily meditations and rituals using crystals and tea.
- ❖ A grimoire of everyday spells that blend tea magick and crystal grids.
- ❖ An exploration of advanced crystal grids for Lunar, Esbat, and Elemental ceremonies.
- ❖ Recipes for crystal elixirs and the energetic qualities of the twelve stones to use to best create them.
- ❖ Appendices to provide you with magickal and intentional correspondences that relate to a wide variety of herbs and crystals.

Ultimately, my intention for this book is to inspire you to embrace the transformative power of these ancient practices, allowing them to guide you on a journey that transcends the mundane acts we live each day and unlock the extraordinary power that lies within you.

Personalizing and Evolving Your Tea and Crystal Grid Practice

Once you explore and further practice tea magick and crystal grid work, you'll discover the true power that is within yourself. Your practice will become personalized and evolve over time to what feels right to your own unique energetic signature and to what aligns with your own magickal journey.

While the tea recipes and rituals in this book provide a solid foundation, personal intuition is your greatest guide. Start by experimenting with different teas, herbs, and infusions that resonate with you personally. If a certain herb or blend calls to you, explore its energies and how it interacts with your own. Begin creating and having fun with your own tea blends. Consider the properties of each herb and how it complements your intentions. For example, if you seek to enhance your clarity and focus, you might blend rosemary for mental clarity with green tea for energy. Always keep a journal of your blends, noting the effects and any adjustments you might make in the future. Tailor your tea brewing rituals to fit your personal energy and intentions. This can include the choice of teaware, the phase of the moon, or even the time of day. Create a ritual that feels uniquely yours, whether it involves reciting personal affirmations, meditating before sipping your tea, or visualizing your goals as you drink.

Please note that this book is not meant to be a comprehensive overview of crystals; it is a guidebook and grimoire to teach you how to incorporate crystals into your tea magick. Not every crystal is included or discussed here, and I encourage you to read and research outside sources to learn more. That said, there are twelve crystals that I

find particularly powerful, especially in healing and well-being work: agate, amethyst, aventurine, black obsidian, carnelian, citrine, clear quartz, jasper, moonstone, rose quartz, smoky quartz, and tiger's eye. I discuss these in detail in the chapter on Crystal Elixirs for Magickal Intent beginning on page 211.

When it comes to crystal grids, I have provided many examples of specific grid layouts for specific intentions—you'll find these in the recipes portion of this book. These will get you started on the crystal tea grid path, but as you grow and expand in your practice, allow your intuition to create new grid patterns and guide you in the choice and placement of crystals. This can lead to profound personal revelations and energetic alignments. Start with a central crystal that aligns with your main intention and intuitively place other stones in a way that feels energetically harmonious to you.

You can also enhance your crystal grids by incorporating symbols, sigils, or objects that carry personal significance. These items can amplify the energy of your grid and deepen the connection to your intentions. Let your crystal grid practice evolve with the natural cycles of the earth and your life. Change your grid with the seasons, aligning your intentions with the energies of each time of year. As your personal goals and circumstances change, update your grid to reflect your current path and aspirations.

Remember to always deepen your practice. Keep a journal of your tea magick and crystal grid experiences in order to track your progress and help you recognize patterns and messages from the universe. Reflect on your feelings, insights, and the outcomes of your practices. Expand your knowledge and respectfully explore different cultures, traditions, and modern practices when it comes to tea and

crystals. This can inspire new elements in your own practice and offer fresh perspectives on how to align your energy work with the universal energies. Most of all, share your experiences and practices with a community that deeply enriches your own journey. Engage with others who walk similar paths, exchange knowledge, and celebrate the diversity and unity within the practices of tea and crystal grid work.

You will find your tea and crystal grid practice to be a journey of self-discovery, intuition, and deep connection with the energies around you. By embracing your unique path and allowing your practices to grow and change with you, you will unlock a powerful tool for transformation and manifestation. Remember, the most beautiful magick is found within the exploration of your inner power and the boundless energies of the universe.

The Art of Brewing

Let us explore and understand the history and cultural significance of tea that will take us on a captivating journey through time, unveiling the rich tapestry of traditions, ceremonies, and spiritual connections that have woven themselves into the very fabric of our world. Dating back thousands of years, the story of tea is one that intertwines with the narratives of ancient civilizations, from its mystical origins in China to its eventual spread across continents. Throughout history, tea has been celebrated not only for its delightful flavors but also for its medicinal properties and its ability to bring people together in moments of shared tranquility and reflection.

The cultural significance of tea spans across diverse societies and traditions. From the elaborate tea ceremonies of Japan, where every gesture holds profound meaning, to the comforting rituals of afternoon tea in the United Kingdom, each culture has woven its own unique narrative around the art of tea-making. Through these traditions, tea has become a symbol of hospitality, mindfulness, and spiritual connection, transforming a mere beverage into a conduit for shared experiences and profound intentions.

Understanding the history and cultural significance of tea allows us to appreciate its role as more than just a drink; it is a bridge between the past and the present, a vessel for intention, and a source of inspiration for the soul. As we explore the depths of tea magick, we honor not just the leaves in our cup but also the centuries of wisdom and tradition that have shaped this humble brew into a potent symbol of harmony and connection.

The world of tea holds many diverse varieties, each with its own unique flavors, aromas, and most especially energetic magickal properties. From the delicate healing notes of white tea, the robust grounding richness of pu-erh, to the expansive folk properties of numerous herbal plants, the spectrum of tea offers an expansive canvas for exploring the interconnectedness of intention, energetic influence, and magickal power.

Most common types of tea—including white tea, green tea, black tea, oolong, pu-erh—all come from the same plant, *Camellia sinensis*. Whether the plant ends up creating a white, green, or black tea depends on how it is processed, or fermented. This is not fermentation in the true sense of the word but rather a process of oxidation—how the leaves are activated by exposure to air and moisture after the leaf is picked from the plant. The different types and lengths of exposure create the resulting color and flavor of the brewed dry leaves. Black teas are oxidized the longest, whereas white teas are barely oxidized at all. Pu-erh tea is aged as well as going through an additional oxidization process. The aging of the tea, which can range from six months to a year, provides its extra depth and smoothness.

White Tea

Known for its subtle and delicate flavors, white tea is revered for its gentle, almost ethereal qualities. Energetically, white tea is often associated with purity, clarity, wisdom, and new beginnings, making it a favored choice for cleansing aura-repairing rituals, lunar ceremonies, and meditation or psychic practices. It is also been appreciated for its fertility, happiness, and protection properties. White tea connects with the energies of Spring and is associated with the colors white, yellow, and gold.

Brewing temperature: 175 degrees F (80 C)
Brewing time: 2 to 4 minutes
Hot: 1.5 teaspoons
Cold: 3 teaspoons

Green Tea

Celebrated for its fresh, grassy notes and invigorating properties, green tea holds a special place in tea culture. Energetically, green tea embodies vitality, growth, and renewal, making it a popular choice for rituals focused on cleansing for personal development, healing, and rejuvenation. It is found in immortality and longevity ceremonies, as well as in spells for passion and love. Because of its rich green color, green tea may be incorporated into money charms too. Green tea is associated with the Summer season and is connected to the colors orange and green.

Brewing temperature: 175 degrees F (80 C)
Brewing time: 45 seconds to 2 minutes
Hot: 1 teaspoon
Cold: 2 teaspoons

Oolong Tea

Oolong tea, with its nuanced flavors and captivating aromas, straddles the line between green and black teas. Energetically, oolong tea is often linked to balance, harmony, and transition, making it an ideal choice for rituals focused on meditation, reflection, equilibrium, and transformation. Due to its brilliant ways of centering and sharpening concentration, it is a wonderful tea to use for divination and wisdom. Because of its balancing and harmonious energy, it also makes it ideal to use for friendship and romance spells. Oolong is connected to the Autumn season and is associated with colors of purples and blues.

Brewing temperature: 195 degree F (90 C)
Brewing time: 3 minutes
Hot: 1 teaspoon
Cold: 2 teaspoons

Black Tea

Adored for its bold flavor and robust character, black tea exudes warmth and depth. Energetically, black tea is often associated with grounding, strength, courage, and stability, making it a favored companion for rituals centered on fortitude and resilience. It is also extremely powerful for ceremonies of banishments and exorcism. Its bold energies make it reliable for money and prosperity spells. It is connected to the Winter season, making its colors black and red.

Brewing temperature: 195 to 205 degrees F (90 – 96 C)
Brewing time: 2 to 3 minutes
Hot: 1 teaspoon
Cold: 2 teaspoons

Pu-Erh Tea

Pu-Erh has always held a sacredness to itself, from how it is grown, cared for, rolled, sun-dried, compressed, and aged through a microbial fermentation process. It is the champagne of tea that can be grown in only one region of the world—Yunan Province, China. It is the finest, oldest, and most pure tea. Because of this, it is held in such high regard that it is ideal for sacred ceremonies of dedication, initiations, and spirit or deity connections. It has powerful earth energies, thus making it ideal for any kind of banishment rituals, honoring the dead, inspiring wisdom, and psychic development. It carries the energies of both earth and sky. Its associated colors are brown and gray.

Brewing temperature: 195 to 200 degrees F (90 – 95 C)
Brewing time: 4 to 5 minutes
Hot: 1 teaspoon
Cold: 2 teaspoons

Herbal Infusions

The world of herbal infusions encompasses a vast assortment of botanical blends, each offering its own unique magickal and energetic properties. From the empowering ginger to the love-inducing rosebuds, herbal infusions cater to a wide range of intentions, including protection, luck, and healing. Understanding the energetic properties of different types of herbal teas allows practitioners to align their intentions with the inherent qualities of each herb, infusing their rituals and moments of mindfulness with purpose and resonance. Whether seeking tranquility, prophetic

dreams, courage, or transformation, the world of tea offers a diverse palette of energetic influences, inviting individuals to explore the profound connections between intention, manifestation, and magick in their practice.

Consult the correspondences provided in the appendices at the back of this book (see page 236) to find the herbs associated with your intention and magick. In the chapter "The Synergy of Tea Magick and Crystal Grids" we will further look at how to find complementary crystal pairing for any herbal tea—for example, you will want to keep in mind colors and energetic influences between crystal and herb.

Selecting Teas for Magickal Purposes

Selecting and sourcing teas for magickal purposes is a thoughtful and enriching ritualistic process that involves not only the consideration of flavors and aromas but also the energetic resonance of each tea variety. When choosing teas for ritualistic and magickal practices, it is essential to seek out high-quality, ethically sourced teas that align with your intentions and spiritual goals.

When selecting teas for magickal purposes, consider the following factors:

Homegrown or Store-Bought: This solely depends upon personal preference. If you have the room in your home to grow your favorite tea herbs, then these herbs will of course be closer to you and familiar with your energy. Foraged herbs carry more of a wild essence and more time may be required to connect and bond with them, all of which can be done during the preparation and drying process. With store-bought, this will require one to truly seek a dependable source. Store-bought tea can be lacking in energy, but this can be remedied when you are working with it by giving it your breath of life. *Your* energy. However, if you find a reliable seller, such as an apothecary or an organic grower, then this can make the store-bought herbs and tea far more likely to be easier to work with. When sourcing teas for magickal purposes, explore reputable tea merchants, local tea shops, or online suppliers that specialize in high-quality, loose-leaf teas. Look for transparent sourcing practices and a commitment to ethical and sustainable production methods. Look for teas and herbs that are sustainably and ethically harvested, organic, and free from additives, as this will help align your practice with great energetic potential.

Intention: Always begin any ritual process by clarifying your intention for the ceremony or practice. Whether you seek happiness, power, health, or spiritual insight, your intention will guide the selection process when it comes to which tea or herbs to use.

Intuitive Connection: Trust your intuition when selecting tea leaves and herbs. Allow yourself to be drawn to certain plants or scents that resonate with your intentions. Your intuition can serve as a powerful guide, helping you choose the botanicals that align most harmoniously with your desired outcome.

Elemental Associations: Consider the elemental associations of the tea leaves and herbs. Each element—Earth, Air, Fire, and Water— carries its own energy and symbolism. For instance, earthy herbs like

patchouli or vetiver may be associated with grounding and stability, while peppermint or eucalyptus can invoke the airy energy of clarity and communication. (See Appendix C on p. 256 for a listing of herbs by elemental qualities.)

Color Magick: Explore the colors associated with different herbs and tea leaves. Color symbolism can greatly enhance your intention. For example, green tea leaves may represent growth, abundance, and healing, while red rooibos tea may symbolize passion and vitality.

Seasonal and Lunar Influences: Consider the seasonal and lunar influences when choosing tea leaves and herbs. Certain plants align with specific seasons or moon phases, amplifying their magickal properties. For instance, during the autumn season, you might incorporate spices like cinnamon or nutmeg for warmth and transformation, while in spring, you may feel drawn to hibiscus or yerba maté for love and energy.

Personal Associations: Reflect on your personal associations and experiences with certain plants. Perhaps you have fond memories of a particular herb from childhood or feel a deep connection to a specific tea leaf. These personal associations can add a layer of personal meaning and power to your tea-brewing rituals.

By carefully selecting and sourcing teas for magickal purposes, practitioners can create a harmonious and intentional connection between the physical and energetic aspects of tea, infusing their rituals and practices with mindfulness, purpose, and resonance. But remember this: tea magick is a highly personal practice and there are no hard and fast rules. Trust your intuition, experiment with different combinations, and observe how each tea blend affects your energy and intentions. As you deepen your understanding of the magickal properties and correspondences of tea leaves and herbs, you will develop a unique and powerful relationship with these botanical allies, enhancing your practice.

Preparation Techniques for Ritual and Meditation

How you prepare your tea for ritual and meditation will be deeply rooted in mindfulness and intention, thus elevating the act of making and consuming tea to a spiritual practice. The careful and deliberate approach to tea preparation not only enhances the flavors and aromas of the tea but also creates a sacred space for introspection, contemplation, and connection with the present moment.

Here are some tea preparation techniques tailored for ritual and meditation:

Mindful Selection: Begin by mindfully selecting the tea that aligns with your intention for the ritual or meditation. Consider the energetic properties of the tea and how they resonate with your spiritual goals.

Cleansing: Before brewing the tea, consider cleansing the tea tools and the space in which you will prepare and consume the tea. This can

be done through smudging, visualization, or other cleansing rituals to create a sacred atmosphere. Utilizing a teakettle is a simple yet effective way to also cleanse the space. Allowing the kettle's whistle to blow as it boils the water banishes negative energies and welcomes good spirits to guide your intentions.

Intention Setting: As you blend and measure out the tea leaves or herbal blends, infuse them with your intention. Visualize your desired outcome and imbue the tea with the energy of your purpose.

Brewing Ritual: Engage in a slow, deliberate brewing process. Whether steeping the tea in a teapot or a simple cup, pay attention to each step—from adding the water to observing the leaves unfurl. Let the brewing process become a meditative act as this will also serve to visually and intentionally see your purpose come to life.

Fragrance Ritual: As the tea steeps, allow the aroma to envelop you. Breathe deeply and let the scent of the tea awaken your senses, grounding you in the present moment.

Serving with Reverence: Pour the tea with reverence, acknowledging the journey from leaf to cup. As you serve the tea, do so mindfully, infusing the act with gratitude and intention.

Sip Mindfully: When you finally taste the tea, do so with full awareness. Let each sip be a moment of connection with the intentions, the desired outcome, and the energies between yourself and the tea spell. By embracing these intentional tea preparation techniques, practitioners can transform the simple act of making tea into a more meaningful ritual of mindfulness and spiritual connection. Each step in the process becomes an opportunity for intention, visualization, and energy manipulation, allowing for the cultivation of a deeper connection with the transformative power of tea.

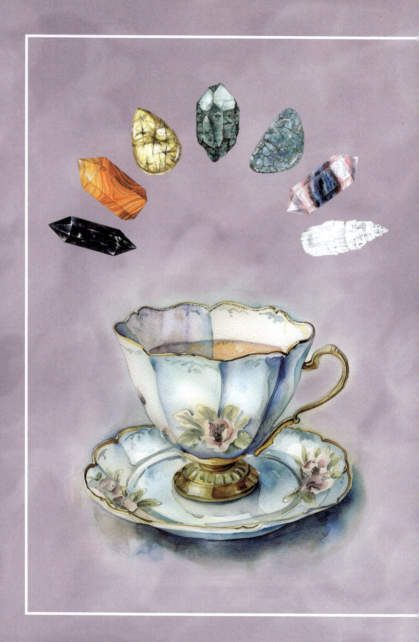

Crystal Magick: Unveiling the Power of Gemstones

Introduction to crystals and their metaphysical properties opens the door to a world of ancient wisdom, energetic connection, and spiritual transformation. Crystals have captivated human imagination for millennia, revered for their beauty, rarity, and purported ability to harness and channel subtle energies.

Metaphysically, crystals are believed to possess unique energetic properties that can influence the environment and the individuals who interact with them. These properties are often associated with the crystal's color, structure, and mineral composition, giving rise to a diverse array of metaphysical attributes.

Here are some key metaphysical properties often associated with crystals:

Energy Amplification: Crystals are said to have the ability to amplify and channel energy. They can enhance the energetic qualities of an environment or an individual, making them valuable tools for intention setting and manifestation.

Healing Properties: Many crystals are believed to possess healing properties, whether for physical, emotional, or spiritual ailments. Different crystals are associated with specific healing intentions, such as promoting relaxation, boosting vitality, or aiding in emotional balance.

Vibrational Resonance: Crystals are thought to vibrate at specific frequencies, and their resonance can influence the energetic field around them. This resonance is often linked to the chakra system and can be used to balance and align the body's energy centers.

Intention Channeling: Crystals are often used as conduits for intention and focus. They can be programmed with specific intentions and are believed to hold and transmit these intentions over time.

Spiritual Connection: Crystals are revered for their ability to facilitate spiritual connection and meditation. They are used in various spiritual practices to enhance intuition, access higher consciousness, and strengthen a deeper connection with the divine.

As we delve into the world of crystals and their metaphysical properties, we embark on a journey that transcends the physical realm, tapping into the profound interplay of energy, intention, and spiritual resonance. Crystals offer a gateway to exploring the subtle energies that permeate our world, inviting us to embrace the transformative potential of these ancient and enigmatic treasures.

Selecting Crystals for Intentions

Selecting crystals for specific intentions involves aligning the energetic properties of the crystals with the desired outcomes of your spiritual practice. Whether you seek to manifest abundance, promote emotional healing, or enhance spiritual connection, understanding the metaphysical properties of crystals and how colors play a role in the selection process can help you choose the most suitable stones for your intentions. Please refer to Appendix B on p. 247 for a list of magickal and intentional correspondences for crystals. Here's a color guide for selecting crystals based on specific color and intentions:

BLACK

Known to be strong protective crystals. They trap negative energies that are then either transmuted or neutralized into positive vibrations. For this, they can be used to detoxify a person, place, or situation. They are also ideal stones to identify lost or hidden gifts and potential that one has not been made fully aware of. These crystals can be used for grids to ground, protect, or reveal hidden potentials.

BLUE

Blue crystals carry strong spiritual energies. They resonate closely with the throat and third eye, and thus stimulate self-expression, clear communication, and connecting to a higher state of consciousness. These crystals stimulate and heighten intuition and channeling. Blue crystal grids activate intuition and metaphysical abilities.

BROWN

Deeply connected to earth energy, brown crystals are ideal for grounding, cleansing, protection, and purifying. They have strong absorbing properties that can take on toxic and negative energies and converts them to stabilizing and focused states. These stones are ideal for long-term grid work, but must be cleansed regularly.

CLEAR OR WHITE

These particular crystals vibrate on a pure light and higher frequency. They are associated with the crown chakra due to its ability to connect you to your higher consciousness. These crystals are often used to purify and link to the higher realms and divinity. They are used especially to cleanse, purify, or open doorways. They are powerful and radiate energy outward into the space and environment; because of this, they are great for grids to heal and purify either the environment, situation, aura, or physical body.

COMBINATION AND BICOLORED

These types of crystals vibrate on a high energetic frequency, thus making them ideal to raise the vibrations of other crystals that are close by. Use in a grid to empower the intentions and purpose. Ideal for fast-acting grids.

GOLD

Known for being the ideal crystals for abundance and manifestation, gold-colored crystals are great for generating positive energies and achieving higher consciousness or enlightenment. These crystals are ideal for grids that are meant to draw prosperity, luck, or long-term success into your life.

GREEN

Green crystals are known to help and connect with the heart chakra. They are very calming and cleansing crystals, providing great emotional healing and instilling tranquility and self-compassion. They form a natural link between heaven and earth. Use green crystals in grids meant to bring calming energies, healing, balancing emotions, and fortune.

GREEN-BLUE AND TURQUOISE

These colored crystals resonate with cosmic and metaphysical properties. They instill a strong, peaceful, and relaxing aura and stimulate spiritual awareness. These crystals are used to connect a bridge between the heart and intuition, bringing balance to the heart and third-eye chakras.

INDIGO

Indigo crystals hold strong connections to the deep depths of spiritual consciousness and the far reaches of space. They can be used to awaken spiritual and psychic abilities, enhance divination, align the chakras, and reach a higher power and calling.

LAVENDER, LILAC, AND PURPLE

Lavender and violet crystals carry light and fine vibrations that make them ideal for meditation and intuitive awareness. Purple crystals resonate with the higher crown chakras and help nudge you into other multidimensional realms of reality. They raise spiritual energy and encourage deep empathic or telepathic connections.

MAGENTA

Much like the purple crystals, magenta crystals also carry high vibrations and stimulate the crown chakras, particularly to the

soul star and causal vortex. They are ideal for divination practices, especially tarot and scrying. They help with grids designed to connect directly to spirit and ancestors.

ORANGE

These colored crystals vibrate and attract abundance, happiness, joy, vitality, creativity, and assertiveness, and build up energetic structures. Orange crystal grids are ideal for starting new projects and new goals, and to open roads.

PEACH

Peach stones are great love stones as they unite both the heart and sacral chakras. They can be used in grids meant to bring two people together, make friendships stronger, or help a situation to move forward.

PINK

These crystals are gentle and light, yet also are wonderful in attracting positive energies into one's life. They symbolize pure, unconditional love and promote forgiveness. They bring comfort and alleviate stress and anxiety, thus making them great for emotionally healing, and mending a broken heart. They are wonderful in grids meant to heal, especially from loss and grief, as well as attracting what is needed into your life. Great for long-term grids of this nature.

RED

Red crystals are connected to the root and sacral chakras, making them ideal for strengthening and activating passion, creativity, and energy. Because of this, they make very effective and powerful crystals, ideal for short-term grids, but must be used wisely, especially when it comes to emotions, as they may overstimulate them. They are good for improving feelings of safety and security.

SILVER-GRAY

Metallic and silvery-gray crystals are unique and can transmute energy. They can convert negative energy into positive. They are deeply connected to the earth and are wonderful for shadow work. They are especially great crystals for overcoming childhood trauma, ancestral wounds, and past life karma, thus also making them great for grounding and protection around a grid.

YELLOW

These crystals help balance the mind and heart, instilling focus and clarity, which also makes them great for reducing stress, anxiety, and depression, and bringing forth warmth, understanding, and balance.

When selecting crystals for specific intentions, it's essential to trust your intuition and choose stones that resonate with you on a personal level. Whether you are drawn to the color, texture, or energetic vibration of a crystal, your connection with the stone is a significant factor in its effectiveness for your intentions. By carefully selecting crystals that align with your spiritual goals, you can create a harmonious and powerful energy field that supports your journey of practice and transformation.

Cleansing, Charging & Programming

Cleansing, charging, and programming your crystals are essential practices to maintain the energetic purity and potency of these sacred stones. Whether you have just acquired a new crystal or wish to reset the energy of a well-loved stone, these rituals help to refresh and attune the crystals to your intentions and energy field. Here's a guide to cleansing, charging, and programming crystals:

CLEANSING

Cleansing involves purifying a crystal to remove any accumulated energy and reset it to its natural state. There are several methods for cleansing crystals:

Water: If the crystals are not layered, fragile, or soluble, and don't have tiny crystals on their matrix, rinse the crystal under running water, visualizing the impurities washing away and the crystal being cleansed by the flow of water. Water may also be made into a clearing essence spray to spritz across the crystals.

Smoke Cleansing: Pass the crystal through the smoke of sacred herbs such as rosemary, bay leaves, sweetgrass, or incense to clear the energy around it. You may also use a purifying simmer pot or singing bowl.

Salt: Place the crystal in a bowl of sea salt or bury it in salt for a few hours to absorb any negative energies. If it is a crystal that easily degrades in salt, it may be placed in brown rice or buried in the ground.

Crystal Cleansing Essence Spray Recipe

Smoky quartz

Black tourmaline

Spring water

Small glass bowl

Small glass bottle

Frankincense essential oil

Vodka

Ensure that all crystals have been cleansed prior to making this spray.

Hold them in your hands and infuse your intentions into the crystals, asking them to cleanse any crystals, grid, person, or space.

Place the crystals in the glass bowl and cover with spring water. It is wise to use fresh water from a pure source. Try to avoid using tap water unless absolutely necessary.

Place the bowl in sunlight for a few hours. Cover if necessary. Afterwards, place the bowl in moonlight for a few hours.

Remove the crystals and use a funnel to pour the water into your glass bottle. Fill it one-third full.

Add a few drops of frankincense oil, then top off the bottle with vodka.

Label the bottle with the date and contents. This can be used and preserved for up to several months.

CHARGING

Charging is the process of infusing a crystal with energy, often before a grid is set and weekly after a grid is made, especially if the energy feels depleted or stagnant. Here are some common charging methods:

Sunlight: Place the crystal in direct sunlight for a few hours, allowing it to absorb the revitalizing energy of the sun. Do this only with crystals that will not lose their color in the sun.

Moonlight: Leave the crystal under the light of the full moon for a few hours, to absorb the gentle, feminine energy associated with lunar cycles.

Earth: Bury the crystal in the soil or place it on the ground to connect with the grounding and stabilizing energy of the earth.

Charging Crystals: Placing crystals on large, energizing crystals such as quartz, selenite, or carnelian will also charge crystals.

Charging Spray: Ready-made charging essence spray to charge or recharge your crystals.

Crystal Charging Essence Spray Recipe

Carnelian

Selenite (use tumbled)

Spring water

Small glass bowl

Small glass bottle

Bay essential oil

Vodka

Ensure that all crystals have been cleansed prior to making this spray.

Hold them in your hands and infuse your intentions into the crystals, asking them to cleanse any crystals, grid, person, or space.

Place the crystals in the glass bowl and cover with spring water. It is wise to use fresh water from a pure source. Try to avoid using tap water unless necessary.

Place the bowl in sunlight for a few hours. Cover if necessary. Afterwards, place the bowl in moonlight for a few hours.

Remove the crystals and use a funnel to pour the water into your glass bottle. Fill it one-third full.

Add a few drops of bay oil, then top off the bottle with vodka.

Label the bottle with the date and contents. This can be used and preserved for up to several months.

PROGRAMMING

Programming a crystal involves setting a specific intention or purpose for the crystal to amplify. To program a crystal:

Hold the crystal in your hands and focus on your intention, visualizing it as a clear and specific outcome.

Speak your intention aloud or silently, infusing the crystal with your purpose and clarity of intention.

Trust your intuition and allow the crystal to attune to your energy and the programmed intention.

By regularly performing these practices, you can maintain the energetic integrity of your crystals and ensure that they remain aligned with your intentions. Whether you are using crystals for meditation, healing, or spiritual rituals, these cleansing, charging, and programming rituals help to create a harmonious and resonant energy exchange between you and the crystals, enhancing their metaphysical properties and supporting your spiritual journey.

Crystal Grids for
Your Magickal Brews

U nderstanding the basic foundation of a grid revolves around having a center stone for focus and a single perimeter of stones arranged into a prechosen geometric pattern. More complex powerful advanced grids can have many detailed layouts with multiple layers, some even incorporating non-crystals, such as herbs, flowers, shells, or meaningful objects and tools.

Focus Stone

When it comes to any grid layout, there is a focus stone that is also called the center stone. These stones act as an anchor for the grid that maintains and powers the main intention. To choose a focus stone, it is all about understanding and knowing what the intention and need are for the grid. For example, if the grid is for protection, then knowing what kind of protection is needed and the feelings going into it will help you decide on the best stone for the occasion, such as black tourmaline or obsidian.

Desire Stones

These type of stones form the layers surrounding the focus stone. These may be a single layer or several, depending on the level of grid you are creating and intuition. Desire stones are meant to fine-tune and boost the power of your focus stone. For example, if you were to choose a carnelian as a focus stone to boost creativity, then you could choose blue lace agate as your desire stones to bring this creativity out through physical expression and action.

Directional Stones

These stones help direct the grid's energy where you want your intentions to go. These stones often are a single layer forming outside of the perimeter. Oftentimes, directional stones are points, triclinic, or stones that are great for perimeters. For example, points can direct energy outwards or inwards depending upon where the point is facing. Triclinic stones help contain the energy within the grid space. Perimeter stones like selenite or smoky quartz can cleanse or change the energy of the grid, allowing them to hold positive space or the energy structure for longer periods of time.

Sacred Geometry

Exploring the principles of sacred geometry in crystal grids unveils a profound and harmonious interplay between the natural patterns of the universe and the energetic properties of crystals. Sacred geometry, which encompasses symbolic and mathematical patterns found in nature and spiritual traditions, serves as a guiding framework for constructing purposeful and resonant crystal grids. By aligning the principles of sacred geometry with the metaphysical attributes of crystals, practitioners can create powerful energetic structures that amplify intentions, manifest desires, and support spiritual growth.

CIRCLES

Circles are the ultimate symbol of oneness and the infinite flow of energy. They symbolize harmony, divinity, birth, life, death, and rebirth. These are the simplest grids that can be made. They send energy outward. You may need five or more stones to create a circle grid. Circles can be used for protection and renewal; to ground energy; to circulate energy; to create healing; to balance the mind, body, and spirit; to attract your desire; to connect to a higher power; to connect with your ancestors.

FLOWER OF LIFE AND SEED OF LIFE

The Flower of Life or the Seed of Life is a symbol composed of overlapping circles, symbolizing the interconnectedness of all living things. The Flower of Life is sometimes represented as a more complex set of overlapping circles than the Seed of Life. Both are shown here. The grid I often use (shown in the illustration on page 36) is an expanded variation of the Seed of Life. These grids resonate with the unity of life and the universal energy flow, amplifying the intentions of the grid. It is created for divine guidance, connecting to the source of energy, expanding power, spiritual growth, creating new ideas, and promoting positive healthy relationships, careers, or any aspect of life. Typically, nineteen crystals may be needed for this grid.

LEMNISCATE

The lemniscate, also known as the infinity symbol, represents the balance of forces and the interconnectedness of all things. The lemniscate brings equilibrium and harmony and is a powerful grid for healing. You can use anywhere from three to eleven crystals for this grid.

MERKABA/STAR TETRAHEDRON

The merkaba is a variation on the Star of David/Hexagram. It is a shape made of two overlapping tetrahedrons. The merkaba creates a powerful energy field that provides protection and can raise your consciousness to a higher, divine level. It represents perfectly balanced opposing energies: masculine and feminine, earth and cosmos. You may need sixteen crystals for this grid.

METATRON'S CUBE

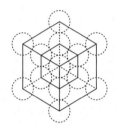

Metatron's Cube is a symbol of balance, harmony, and interconnectedness, known as the "map of the multiverse." This symbol links together all dimensions, the four cardinal directions, and the concept "as above, so below." It symbolizes infinite and finite possible universes. It assists in moving beyond the realms of time and reality, creating inspirations and transforming life—ideal when calling on divine or angelic assistance, in activating your spiritual or psychic abilities, and lastly, in transmuting negative patterns or thoughts into positive ones. Thirteen crystals may be needed for this grid.

PENTAGRAM

A pentagram grid may be encased in a pentagon, or as a star within a circle grid. It can be created to connect to nature, the elements, grounding, manifesting all that you desire, bringing together energy for intense manifestation, protection against negativity, honoring the sabbats, esbats, and other celebrations. It connects the realms. You may need at least eleven stones for a pentagram grid.

SPIRALS

Spirals can be found throughout nature as a lovely symbol of eternal growth and unblocking roads. They radiate outward and can continue to radiate energy infinitely. They represent universal harmony and the connection we share between ourselves and the elements. You can create spiral grids for personal growth, spiritual growth, unfolding paths, and opening new opportunities. Helps to begin a project, or to reenergize a space. You may need seven crystals or as many as you wish to use.

SQUARE/DIAMOND

A square harbors great anchoring and grounding energies. It consolidates energy, balancing and solidifying it. It can be created to make a protective and contained safe space. It can be made for a long-term period. The grid can protect a space, promote healthy sleep, calm the atmosphere, reduce internal stress, and create clarity. Best to use when energy or a situation has lost control and needs to be calmed to be reevaluated. You may need five stones to create this grid.

STAR OF DAVID/HEXAGRAM

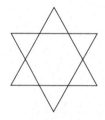

Also known as the "Creator's Star," it is a protective shape and has been used to connect to higher realms. Thus, it has been used to join two halves into a whole and to find unity both in life and within oneself. It is created for protection and wards against negative energy or negative thinking. It helps undo bad habits and patterns. It balances the heart chakra, making it ideal for building kindness, harmony, peace, and love in a home. It attracts a partner either in love or in business. You may need thirteen crystals for this grid.

44

SUNBURSTS

Sunburst grids radiate around the shape of a circle and symbolize passion and energy. They are ideal in directing intentions outward and making things possible. They may also be used for purification and to improve the mind, body, and spirit, bringing clarity and creativity. This grid boosts energy both inwardly and outwardly. It strengthens willpower and intentions, and creates fortune and luck. It promotes positive energy and emotions.

TIBETAN KNOT

The Tibetan knot is a beautiful symbol known as the "endless knot" or "eternal knot." A deeply spiritual symbol, it can be used to create connections between life and nature, spirituality and reality to uncover truths; strengthen the connection between others; heal grief and soul loss; deepen meditations; inspire love; and honor promises or vows. Fifteen crystals may be needed to create this grid.

TREE OF LIFE

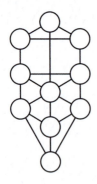

Known as a Kabbalistic symbol, the tree of life can be found and incorporated within the Flower of Life symbol. The tree of life creates a path to universal truth and healing. This symbol represents the ten energy centers: the divine crown, wisdom, understanding, mercy, justice or strength, beauty, victory, splendor, foundation, and the power of physical healing. It can be created to balance the chakras and form connection with a higher power and to the source of energy. Ten crystals may be needed to create this grid.

TRIANGLE

The triangle grid balances and strengthens elemental energies; brings balance and harmony; promotes healing and brings clarity; creates stability, thus making it ideal for smoothing out discord and instilling the strength to overcome. It is excellent for protecting a space. This grid often simply needs four crystals, but more can be used if desired. May also be incorporated into other grids.

TRIQUETRA

A triquetra grid is a symbol of love, faith, friendship, protection, and loyalty. It can be used to bring unity between the mind, body, and spirit. It can be used to help overcome anxiety, stress, and depression. It protects against negativity and breaks destructive patterns and habits, helps to get unstuck from a situation, helps heal and promote health, and attracts wealth and success. You may need at least seven crystals for this grid.

TRISKELION

A triskelion grid is a sacred symbol often being represented as the spiral of life. It symbolizes movement and growth. It honors the cycles of life and time: past, present, and future, or birth, life, and death. It is most ideal to work with this grid for karmic lessons or issues, dealing with grief or honoring a loved one, healing time, and being present. Often, it takes at least thirteen stones to create this grid.

VESICA PISCIS

Composed of two overlapping circles, this grid is known as "the womb of the universe." It inspires great balance in various aspects of

life, creation, fertility, passion, union, creativity, connecting to the universe; creates forgiveness, compromise, and balance between relationships; and addresses any sacral chakra imbalance. Also perfect for starting a new venture. You may need eleven crystals to create a vesica piscis grid.

When constructing a crystal grid based on the principles of sacred geometry, practitioners can choose specific crystals based on their energetic properties and alignment with the intentions of the grid. For example, the square shape confers protection and promotes healthy sleep. If you consult Appendix B (page 247) for correspondences for both protection and sleep, you'll find jade, amber, black tourmaline, amethyst, obsidian, selenite, lepidolite, labradorite, smoky quartz, and moonstone, among many others. By embracing the principles of sacred geometry in crystal grids, practitioners can tap into the innate harmony and resonance of the natural world, creating powerful tools for their own personal transformation, craft, and spiritual practice. The integration of sacred geometry and crystal energy in grid work offers a profound pathway to harmonizing the physical and energetic realms, fostering a deeper curiosity toward the connection with the universal forces that underpin existence.

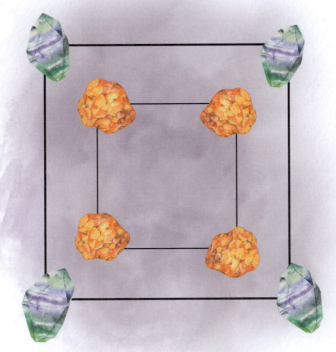

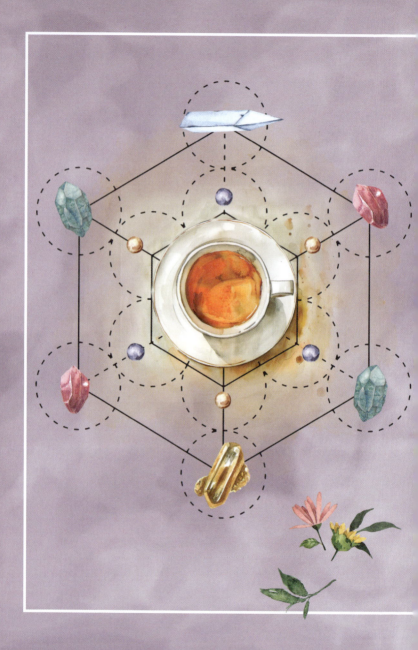

The Synergy of Tea Magick and Crystal Grids

The energetic connection between tea and crystals unveils a harmonious interplay between two ancient and revered sources of natural energy. Both tea and crystals have long been utilized for their profound metaphysical properties, and when combined, they create a synergistic union that can enhance spiritual practices, mindfulness, and energetic manipulation.

The energetic connection between tea and crystals can be explored through several key pathways:

Intention Setting: Both tea and crystals can be used as tools for intention setting and manifestation. When preparing a cup of tea, one can infuse the whole process, from the water to the tea leaves, with specific intentions, much like programming a crystal and a grid with a purpose. The combined energy of the intentional tea and the resonant crystals creates a potent field of focused energy aligned with the practitioner's desires.

Energetic Frequency: Crystals are believed to radiate specific energetic frequencies, and when placed near or in contact with tea, they influence the energetic properties of the beverage. The subtle vibrations of the crystals harmonize with the energetic essence of the tea, enhancing its transformative and healing qualities.

Ritual and Mindfulness: Both tea ceremonies and crystal rituals are steeped in mindfulness, intentionality, and sacred practice. When combined, they create a space for heightened spiritual awareness, introspection, and connection with the universal energies. The act of preparing and holding space with tea in the presence of crystals can elevate the experience to a meditative and transformative ritual, moving intentions into reality.

Energetic Cleansing and Charging: Just as crystals benefit from cleansing and charging, tea leaves and herbs can absorb and hold on to energetic imprints. Placing crystals near tea during brewing can contribute to the energetic cleansing and charging of the tea, infusing it with focused and empowering energy.

Amplification of Energies: The combined energies of tea and crystals have the potential to amplify the intentions and energetic qualities of each other. This synergy creates a vibrant and resonant energy exchange, enhancing the overall vibrational qualities of both the tea and the crystals.

By embracing and exploring the energetic connection between tea and crystals, practitioners can create a sacred and transformative space for enlightenment, magick, and energetic connection. Whether through the practice of brewing tea in the presence of crystals, incorporating crystal grids into tea rituals, or infusing tea with the intentionality of specific crystals, the union of tea and crystals offers a unique and powerful avenue for spiritual connection and energy exploration.

Matching Your Tea with Crystals

The correspondences between teas and crystals are a fascinating exploration of the complementary energies and metaphysical properties of these ancient and revered sources of natural energy. By aligning the unique qualities of specific teas with the energetic attributes of corresponding crystals, practitioners can create harmonious and resonant combinations that support the practice and discover the best pairings for tea and crystals. Here's a guide to some of the best pairings between favorite common teas and crystals, and while these combinations are helpful, the true connections will come from experimenting and what feels right to your intuition.

WHITE TEA

White, clear, and yellow crystals such as quartz, moonstone, Herkimer diamond, howlite, pearls, white agate, white jasper, white opals, citrine, pyrite, golden healer, yellow apatite, bumblebee jasper, and amber pair wonderfully with this type of tea.

GREEN TEA

Tiger's eye, goldstone, aragonite, orange calcite, amber, sunstone, carnelian, peach moonstone, topaz, fire agate, orange aventurine, malachite, emerald, jade, bloodstone, prehnite, moldavite, serpentine, green aventurine, ruby zoisite, fluorite, unakite, labradorite, chrysocolla, moss agate, and dragon stone pair with this tea.

OOLONG TEA

Crystals such as amethyst, tanzanite, fluorite, kunzite, sapphire, chalcedony, sugilite, charoite, purple agate, rhodolite, purple jasper, sodalite, apatite, blue kyanite, angelite, chrysocolla, larimar, lapis lazuli, turquoise, aquamarine, and amazonite pair lovely with this tea.

BLACK TEA

Crystals such as black obsidian, black tourmaline, onyx, hematite, black moonstone, jet, red aventurine, garnet, ruby, red jasper, red tiger's eye, and red agate pair powerfully with black tea.

PU-ERH TEA

Crystals such as smoky quartz, tiger iron, brown agate, tiger's eye, bronzite, chiastolite, agate, snowflake obsidian, and gray chalcedony pair nicely with this tea.

EARL GREY TEA

Clear quartz, green aventurine, labradorite, lapis lazuli, blue tiger's eye, amazonite, peridot, moonstone, rose quartz, topaz, tourmaline, smoky quartz, and citrine all make nice pairings

CHAMOMILE TEA

Amethyst, clear quartz, tiger's eye, lapis lazuli, aquamarine, and tanzanite pair nicely with this tea

PEPPERMINT TEA

Clear quartz, tiger's eye, lapis lazuli, carnelian, green aventurine, apatite, labradorite, pyrite, ruby, sapphire, jasper, and agate all pair nicely.

HIBISCUS TEA

Rose quartz, amethyst, red jasper, carnelian, and clear quartz make lovely pairings with this tea.

LAVENDER TEA

Labradorite, amethyst, tiger's eye, hematite, clear quartz, aquamarine, blue calcite, chrysocolla, emerald, opal, moonstone, rose quartz, sapphire, tanzanite, and black obsidian are powerful pairings.

ROSE TEA

Clear quartz, green aventurine, labradorite, rose quartz, emerald, moonstone, ruby, and tanzanite pair lovely with this tea.

JASMINE TEA

Moonstone, jasper, green aventurine, clear quartz, carnelian, emerald, garnet, lapis lazuli, peridot, rose quartz, and topaz pair nicely with this tea.

ROSEMARY TEA

Clear quartz, labradorite, lapis lazuli, topaz, turquoise, and smoky quartz are nice pairings with this tea.

LEMON TEA

Tiger's eye, jasper, lapis lazuli, labradorite, clear quartz, apatite, citrine, chrysocolla, garnet, opal, pyrite, sapphire, sunstone, topaz, and tourmaline make lovely pairings with this tea.

CHAI TEA

Pyrite, carnelian, amethyst, tiger's eye, jasper, clear quartz, hematite, amazonite, apatite, aquamarine, citrine, peridot, ruby, turquoise, moonstone, and black obsidian are powerful pairings with this tea.

By exploring the best pairings between teas and crystals, practitioners can create intentional and resonant remedies that support specific energetic intentions and emotional well-being. Please refer to appendices A and B to find a list of magickal and intentional correspondences for tea, herbs, and crystals. Whether used in tea rituals or meditation practices, the synergistic combination of teas and crystals offers a unique and potent avenue for harnessing the transformative and harmonizing energies within ourselves and of nature.

Creating Intentional Tea Blends

Creating intentional blends and crystal pairings offers a profound way to amplify the energetic properties of both herbal blends and crystals, resulting in a harmonious and resonant synergy that supports specific intentions for your spiritual practices. By carefully selecting herbs and crystals based on their metaphysical properties and aligning them with specific intentions, practitioners can craft intentional blends and crystal pairings that embody the desired energetic qualities. Here's a guide to creating intentional blends and crystal pairings:

SELECTING INTENTIONAL HERBS AND BLENDS

Choose herbs and botanicals based on their metaphysical properties and traditional uses; for example, lavender for relaxation, rose for love and compassion, and lemongrass for purification. Consider the intended purpose of the blend, whether it's promoting relaxation, enhancing focus, fostering emotional healing, or supporting spiritual growth.

ALIGNING CRYSTALS WITH INTENTIONAL BLENDS

Select crystals that resonate with the energetic qualities of the chosen herbs; for example, black obsidian to complement a protection blend, rose quartz for a love-infused blend, or clear quartz to amplify the overall intention of the blend. Consider the color, energetic vibration, and metaphysical correspondences of the crystals in relation to the intended purpose of the blend.

INTENTION SETTING AND RITUAL

Set a clear intention for the intentional blend and crystal pairing, infusing both the herbs and crystals with the desired purpose or outcome. Engage in a ritual or mindfulness practice when preparing and consuming the intentional blend, incorporating the presence of the paired crystals to enhance the energetic experience.

By creating intentional blends and crystal pairings, practitioners can harness the combined energies of herbal infusions and crystals to support their magickal intentions and practices. Whether used for meditation, ritual, or everyday mindfulness, intentional blends and crystal pairings offer a powerful and transformative avenue for aligning with the natural energies of the earth and fostering a deeper connection to intentionality and spiritual resonance.

Preparing for Your Crystal Tea Ritual

Enhancing rituals and meditation practices with combined energies involves harnessing the synergistic power of various elements, such as crystals, essential oils, herbs, and other natural materials, to create a powerful energetic field that supports intention, alignment, and magick. By carefully integrating these elements into rituals and meditation practices, practitioners can amplify the energetic qualities of their spiritual endeavors, fostering a deeper connection to the self and the natural world. Here's a guide to enhancing the rituals and practice with combined energies and tools.

SELECTING INTENTIONAL ELEMENTS

Choose crystals, essential oils, herbs, or other natural materials based on their metaphysical properties and alignment with the intended purpose of the ritual. For example, select citrine for luck, orange essential oil for success, and yellow and orange candles and black tea for wealth. Consider the color, energetic vibration, and correspondences of the chosen elements in relation to the desired outcome of the practice.

ALIGNING WITH THE ELEMENTS

Set a clear intention for the ritual or meditation practice, infusing the chosen elements with the desired purpose or outcome. Engage in a ritual and practice, incorporating the presence of the combined elements to create a sacred and intentional space. Consider the area and space where the ritual is being performed. If you are creating a tea grid for a peaceful home, the element needed would be a hearth; thus the ritual needs to be done in the home. Another example would be if a tea grid is for grounding and balance, then the ritual can be done outside in the garden.

MINDFULNESS AND PRESENCE

Embrace mindfulness and presence when working with the combined energies, allowing the subtle vibrations and resonances of the elements to guide and support the manifestation journey. Cultivate a deep connection to the natural world and the inherent energies of the chosen elements, fostering a sense of grounding, alignment, and attunement. Be ever mindful as you prepare your space and set the kettle, choosing and blending your herbs. Pour the water and experience the stillness as it steeps. Being present helps align the energies, focus the power, thus brewing and manifesting intentions into reality.

Tools for Ritual

Tools are a wonderful way to combine and focus the energies of both the space and oneself. Wield them to manipulate the intention towards the ritual. Consider keeping these tools close at hand or blending them into your own practice when it involves tea and crystal grids.

KNIFE/HERB SCISSORS

Tools for the element of Fire. Carry masculine energies. Often a white handle is best. May be placed in the south end of a tea tray. Help to direct energy within the space. Great for cutting away negative energies, summoning protection, and charging and consecrating herbs.

TEASPOON/SPOONS

Tools for the element of Air. Carry masculine energies. Tools of invocation because they serve as the will of the brewer and summon their energy to the forefront. Used to charge the brew, bestow blessings, draw down energies during ritual, and evoke the spirits, deities, or ancestors. May be placed on the east end of a tea tray. Spoons may be made of wood, metals, heatproof glass, and sometimes water and heat-safe gemstones.

TRIVET/TEA WARMER

Tools for the element of Earth. Carry feminine energies. Grounding tools to calm and balance the energies of the ritual space or aid in protecting the space. May be placed in the north end of a tea tray, but for the purpose of most of the crystal grids in this book, these tools will often be placed at the center. Trivets or tea warmers are typically made of cast iron, ceramic, or glass.

TEAPOT/TEACUP/KETTLE

Tools for the element of Water. Carry feminine energies. Symbolize the containment and the womb of the goddess or sacred energies. Use to bless the sacred waters, brews, and libations for rituals and spells. They are symbolic of inspiration, rebirth, illumination, abundance, manifestation, and rejuvenation, thus, making them the ultimate tools for general conjuring, for they represent not only the element of Water, but also the element of spirit, bringing that which is not yet reality into our physical realm.

TEA TRAY

Tool of all the elements. Carries both masculine and feminine energies. The tea tray creates a space that essentially is the circle of your ritual, uniting all the energies of each magickal tool. Summons a protective boundary and balances the energies. Tea trays may be made from wood, metals, or even gemstones, and carved or painted with sacred symbols. A crystal grid may be set down and activated within a tea tray if it fits.

GEOMETRIC LAYOUT

Tool of all the elements. Carries both masculine and feminine energies. It is important to choose an appropriate layout for your crystal grids. Placing your grid on a cloth, paper sheet, wood, linen, cotton, slate, or stone will help further ground and actualize the energies of the grid. Selecting a color that matches the intention will also enhance the power of the grid. Choosing a layout that also has the geometric pattern of choice imprinted upon it also adds an aid to your practice.

Let's take a closer look at the powerful geometry of crystal grids.

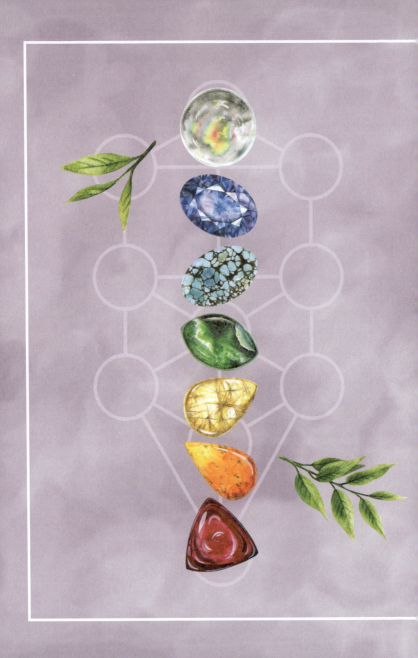

Designing and Activating Crystal Grids

rystal grid layouts are a powerful and intentional arrangement of crystals, designed to amplify and manifest specific intentions, facilitate healing, and support spiritual growth. These layout possibilities are endless. By aligning with these sacred symbols and patterns, practitioners can create potent energetic structures that resonate with the natural harmony of the universe and within themselves.

We've already discussed the importance of choosing the right crystals for your intentions. It is a deeply personal and intuitive process that involves aligning the energetic properties of crystals with specific desires, emotional needs, and spiritual aspirations. We have explored the various shapes in sacred geometry and their meanings. Now, we will take a deep dive into the crystal itself, for not only are we using crystals to construct a grid shape, it is also essential to recognize that crystals have their own unique grid shape *within the stone itself*.

There are seven unique crystal systems—seven unique types of internal lattice structures that can manifest within a crystal. This crystal system is what allows each crystal to carry a unique vibrational quality that can support various aspects of well-being, from emotional healing and manifestation to spiritual growth and energetic protection. By understanding the metaphysical properties of crystals and engaging in a mindful selection process, practitioners can harness the transformative power of crystals.

Understanding Crystal Systems

The internal lattice that is within each crystal is created from atoms that have been packed together. A "family" of crystals will be a group in which the crystals carry the same unique structure—this is regardless of the outer shape, color, or size. All crystals in the family will have the same internal lattice. For example, a sapphire and a ruby are in the same family—trigonal—although one is blue and the other red. The same is true of peridot (green) and tanzanite (usually purple)—both are in the orthorhombic family.

Crystal systems work and channel energy differently according to their inner structure. In addition to the seven main crystal groups, there is an eighth amorphous system that has no internal lattice. The chart on page 67 illustrates the seven shapes so you can follow along. For all you witches who thought you'd never see math again after you finished your childhood schooling, here it is: geometry! However, no worries: we're not going to focus on the math of it, but rather how each of these shapes enhances and contributes to your crystal magick. Here's a guide to choosing the right crystals for your intentions.

AMORPHOUS OR ORGANIC (NO LATTICE)

These crystals have rapid-flowing energy that can be used to grow or release energy, depending upon the intention. They can also radiate and surround a body with energy to protect, cleanse, and release. Solidified natural substances such as amber are amorphous.

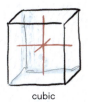

cubic

tetragonal

hexagonal

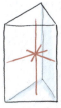

trigonal

orthorhombic

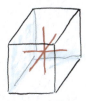

monoclinic

triclinic

HEXAGONAL (RHOMBOHEDRAL)

These crystals add balance and organize energy. They add support especially when it comes to specific issues. Examples shown: beryl, apatite, zincite.

ISOMETRIC (CUBIC)

Cubic crystals create grids for structure, reorganizing, stabilizing, grounding, and cleansing a space. Examples shown: garnet, spinel, pyrite.

MONOCLINIC

These crystals balance and can be used for purification purposes. They also aid in clarity and meditation grids. Examples shown: wolframite, gypsum, orthoclase.

ORTHORHOMBIC

These crystals carry a lot of vibrant and energetic properties, making them ideal for increasing the flow of intentions, and in cleansing and dispelling unwanted energies. Examples shown: barite, sulphur, topaz.

TETRAGONAL

These are powerful transformational crystals that can bring resolution to issues, balance the flow of energy, open and harmonize a purpose and space. Examples shown: aponite, rutile, zircon.

TRICLINIC

Truly a protective type of crystal that helps open perceptions, integrate energies, and heal opposites. Examples shown: wollastonite, rhodonite, albite.

TRIGONAL

These crystals help balance, ground, and focus energy, which then energizes and protects the space and aura. Examples shown: calcite, corundum, quartz.

External Shape Effects

The internal lattice is important, but the external shape holds importance too. And it is, of course, one of the first things you notice about a stone—your intuition is usually drawing you to color and shape. While the outer form does not reflect in the internal lattice, the crystal shape itself can also show how the energy will flow within a grid.

BALL

Crystal balls emit energies equally all around their surface. These crystals make an ideal center stone for a grid that radiates intentions into the surrounding space.

CLUSTER

Clusters contain multiple points on a base that transfers energy in multiple directions, which can make them ideal center stones for grids.

DOUBLE TERMINATED

Crystals that radiate energy from points at both ends. They are wonderful crystals that move energy in both directions when in a grid. They are also great for breaking old patterns.

EGG

These crystals help focus energies. The gentle point can be pointed down in a grid to channel energy into a body or the environment, or pointed up to transfer the energy out.

ELESTIAL

These types of crystals have many windows, or inner planes, and can gently move energy, which can be used to change a perspective. These crystals make wonderful center or anchor stones in grids.

FACETED

These are semiprecious and precious stones that are often cut—faceted—to permit more light into the crystal. While gorgeous to look at, the faceting process does not make them any more important or energetic in a grid.

GENERATOR

Often six-pointed or several-pointed that permit energies in equal directions. These crystals are wonderful in bringing people together, healing, or manifesting.

GEODE

These crystals are great in amplifying, conserving, or slowing manifest intentions; this makes them great for long-term grids. These are great to use in grids meant to help stagnant energy move again, or if energy is moving too fast and needs to be redirected for a different purpose.

MANIFESTATION

These are smaller crystals that have been encased within an outer crystal. These are wonderful manifestation crystals that carry the power to draw in prosperity, abundance, positive energies, and most any other set intentions. For this reason, they make great center stones.

PALMSTONE

These flat and rounded stones help bring calm and balance to the mind, making them perfect for center stones to help focus the intentions of what is most desired.

PHANTOM

These pointed inner pyramid crystals are wonderful for breaking old patterns, healing, and raising vibrations.

POINT

These naturally pointed crystals are ideal to draw in energy or to push away energy, making them ideal for cleansing, purifying, and energizing a grid.

PYRAMID

These crystals create energy and pour it out from the point. They can be used to add protection to a space or person, and also make wonderful center stones in a grid.

RAW

These rough chunks of natural crystals or stones work very well in grids for their natural energetic flow. These are ideal for any kind of healing, grounding, protection, or weather grids.

SCEPTER

These crystals are formed around a central core rod, which makes them ideal for empowering and restructuring and activating a grid.

SQUARE

These crystals ground and anchor intentions. They are especially ideal for drawing away negativity, banishing, and purifying and transforming energy.

TUMBLED

These rounded stones expel energy or can draw in positive energy, making them wonderful for multipurpose grids.

WAND

These are long-pointed crystals that help focus energy, either to draw it in or push away. These are useful when you are joining crystals in a grid and to point the direction.

Intuitive Selection Process

While it is important and ideal to understand how each crystal is unique and powerful, I will always suggest allowing your intuition to guide you. There is no need to feel limited or feel you must buy all the crystals in the world. Sometimes, the best combination of crystals is the ones you have kept for years. Nevertheless, your intuition is your best guide. Engage in a mindful and intuitive selection process when choosing crystals. Allow yourself to be drawn to stones that resonate with your intentions. Trust your intuition and the subtle energetic pull of the crystals, recognizing that your innate wisdom can guide you toward the right stones for your current needs. Consider the energetic compatibility of crystals with your intentions, selecting stones that align with the qualities you seek to cultivate. Pay attention to the emotional and physical responses you experience when handling different crystals, noting any sensations of warmth, vibration, or resonance.

Designing and activating crystal grids is a sacred and intentional process that involves aligning the energetic properties of crystals with specific intentions, geometric patterns, and spiritual symbols. By carefully crafting a grid based on sacred geometry and the principles of intentionality, practitioners can create a potent and resonant energetic structure that supports manifestation and energetic alignment. Here's a step-by-step guide to activating crystal grids:

STEP 1: SET YOUR INTENTION

❖ Clarify the specific intention for your crystal grid, whether it's manifestation, healing, love, protection, or spiritual growth.

❖ Formulate a clear and concise intention statement, expressing your desires and aspirations for the grid's energetic focus. This in turn will guide you in choosing the right crystal for the job.

STEP 2: CHOOSE CRYSTALS

❖ Select crystals that align with your intention, drawing upon their metaphysical properties and energetic qualities.

❖ Consider the symbolism, color, and vibrational resonance of the crystals, choosing stones that support the specific aspects of your intention.

❖ Let your intuition guide you as well. When the right crystal calls to you, it will vibrate, tingle, or go cold or warm. You will feel it in your energy.

STEP 3: SELECT A SACRED SYMBOL OR GEOMETRIC PATTERN

❖ Choose a sacred symbol or geometric pattern to serve as the framework for your crystal grid, such as the Flower of Life, Metatron's Cube, or a specific sacred geometric shape.

❖ The chosen symbol or pattern will guide the arrangement of the crystals and contribute to the overall energetic resonance of the grid.

STEP 4: PREPARE YOUR SACRED SPACE

❖ Create a sacred and intentional space for designing and activating your crystal grid, ensuring a serene and focused environment.

❖ Clear the space with incense, herbs, sprays, sound bowls, or other purifying tools to remove any stagnant or negative energy.

❖ Activate your crystals and awaken them with your intentions. Do this by simply holding the cleansed crystals in your hands, focusing your energy toward them, and stating your purpose for the crystals.

STEP 5: ARRANGE YOUR CRYSTALS

❖ Begin arranging your crystals on a sacred grid cloth or a sacred geometry template, following the chosen geometric pattern or sacred symbol.

❖ Place the crystals with mindful intention, focusing on their alignment with the symbol and the overall energetic flow of the grid. If your grid is intended to draw energy in or to manifest, place the outermost crystals first. If you grid is intended to radiate outward and draw away, place the center stone first.

STEP 6: ACTIVATE THE GRID

❖ Use a clear quartz crystal, a wand, your dominant hand, or your mind to energetically connect the crystals within the grid.

❖ Starting from the center, trace a line connecting each crystal, visually or physically activating the energetic pathways between them.

STEP 7: INFUSE WITH INTENTION

❖ Infuse the crystal grid with your intention by speaking or silently projecting your desired outcome into the grid.

❖ Visualize the grid as a conduit for manifesting your intention, fostering a deep connection between the crystals and your desired energetic focus.

STEP 8: CHARGING AND MAINTENANCE

❖ Place the activated crystal grid in a prominent and sacred space, allowing it to continue radiating its energetic resonance.

❖ Periodically cleanse and recharge the crystals, as well as reaffirm your intention to maintain the grid's potency.

Dismantling a Grid

Once a grid has done its work and served its purpose, it can be dismantled. It is unwise to leave an activated grid running, as it can leave an energetic imprint within the space, which can interfere with future grids you may create. To deactivate a grid, follow these steps:

STEP 1

Hover your hands over the grid and state out loud or within your mind that the grid has fulfilled its purpose, and that the energy may now be put to rest. Express gratitude to the crystals, herbs, and any higher powers or guides that have supported your working.

Use your crystal quartz, wand, or dominant hand to energetically disconnect the crystals within the grid. You may do this in the opposite direction from how you originally laid the crystals.

STEP 2

Cleanse the crystals thoroughly after dismantling. Dark or smoky crystals in particular benefit most to be cleansed in the earth or in brown rice.

Hold the cleansed crystals afterwards and thank them for their work and essence. Ask them to go to sleep and rest until they are needed again.

STEP 3

Recharge your crystals in either sunlight, moonlight, spray essence, or earth for a couple of hours, then place them carefully away.

STEP 4

Cleanse the space in which the grid was laid with either cleansing spray, smudging, or sound. This is to clear away any remaining multilevel energetic imprints.

By following these steps, practitioners can create powerful and purposeful crystal grids that embody their intentions and support their spiritual and energetic endeavors. The intentional design and activation of crystal grids offer a tangible and visually striking representation of one's spiritual aspirations, serving as a potent tool for magick.

Preparing for Ritual

Aligning crystal grids with tea rituals and ceremonies offers a potent combination of energies, intention setting, and magickal manifestation. Tea involves the intentional use of herbal teas, rituals, and ceremonies to support spiritual and magickal intentions. By integrating crystal grids with tea magick, practitioners can create a harmonious and transformative space that fosters a deeper connection to the natural energies of the earth and supports intentionality of their own desires. Here's a guide to aligning crystal grids with tea rituals and ceremonies:

SELECTING INTENTIONAL HERBAL TEAS

Choose herbal teas that align with the specific intentions of your tea ritual, such as happiness, aura renewal, psychic enhancement, or healing. Consider the metaphysical properties of herbs and botanicals, selecting teas based on their energetic resonance with your desired outcome and blending them in perfect balance.

CREATING A SACRED SPACE

Prepare a sacred and intentional space for your tea ritual, ensuring a serene and focused environment for the integration of crystal grids and tea ceremonies. Clear the space with incense, rosemary, cedar, cleansing spray, sound bowls, or other purifying tools to remove any stagnant or negative energy. Prepare the space with the appropriate cleansed tools for the ritual, altar cloth, grid pattern, candles, incense, music, tea tools, tea warmer, teacup, and saucer.

CRAFTING AN INTENTIONAL CRYSTAL GRID

Design and activate a crystal grid that aligns with the intentions of your tea ritual, using sacred symbols, geometric patterns, and specific

crystals that resonate with your desired outcome. Arrange the crystals with mindful intention, infusing them with the energy of your tea ceremony and aligning them with the natural flow of the ritual.

INFUSING THE TEA CEREMONY WITH INTENTION

Brew your chosen tea blend mindfully, infusing the process with your intention and the energetic resonance of the crystal grid. Engage in a simple spell or ceremony, incorporating the presence of the crystal grid to enhance the energetic experience and align with the natural energies of the earth.

MINDFULNESS AND PRESENCE

Embrace mindfulness and presence as you partake in your tea ritual, allowing the subtle vibrations and resonances of the crystal grid and tea brew to guide and support your spiritual journey. Engage in meditation, intention setting, or other spiritual practices while sipping your tea, fostering a deeper connection to intentionality and spiritual alignment.

CLOSING THE SPACE

When the intentions have been set, magickal energies cast, and meditation and tea have been concluded, it is time to close the space. Depending upon the intention of the crystal grid, you may choose to deactivate and dismantle the crystal grid right then. If it is a grid meant for long-term intentions, it may remain activated until it has fulfilled its purpose. Consider how to handle the remnants of your magickal tea blend accordingly.

Crystal tea grids provide practitioners with a potent and transformative space for magickal rituals and ceremonies, meditations, and spells. The integration of crystal grids with tea magick offers a unique and powerful avenue for aligning with the natural energies of the earth and fostering a deeper connection between the elements and the power within yourself. Whether used for meditation, energy work, or sacred remedies, the combination of crystal grids and tea provides a tangible and visually striking representation of one's spiritual aspirations, supporting a deeper connection to the natural world and the inherent energies of self and the earth.

Daily Practice: Meditations and Rituals

Incorporating tea and crystal practices into daily life can offer a harmonious and intentional approach to nurturing well-being, fostering mindfulness, and aligning with the natural energies of the earth. Both tea rituals and crystal practices have a rich history of supporting emotional, physical, and spiritual wellness, and it can be fun and empowering to integrate them into daily everyday routines. In turn, this daily practice can provide grounding and transformative experiences. Consider different ways to incorporate tea and crystal practices into daily life. Here are some suggestions.

Daily Intention Setting

You can begin any day with a mindful tea ritual, selecting a tea that aligns with your intentions for the day, such as focus, energy, or emotional balance. This ritual can go hand in hand with an oracle or tarot pull to determine the best course of intent. Create a small crystal grid on your kitchen table, tea saucer, around the teacup, or countertop, infusing it with the intention of setting a positive and purposeful tone for the day. Embrace and enjoy the energies, being ever mindful of the present moment and your desires.

MEDITATION AND MINDFUL PRACTICES

Crystal grids can be activated and used during meditation or mindfulness practices to enhance spiritual connection and energy alignment. Enjoy a calming cup of herbal tea during meditation, allowing the soothing properties of the tea to support relaxation and inner peace. This will help tune you to the frequencies of internal healing and balance.

WORK AND PRODUCTIVITY SUPPORT

It is incredibly helpful to keep a small crystal grid on your work desk to support focus, creativity, and productivity during the day. It is also amazing to incorporate short tea breaks throughout the day, selecting teas that promote mental clarity, energy, or stress relief, and using these breaks as moments for intentional reflection and rejuvenation. Your tea can be placed within the grid to be infused and further empowered to instill this focus and intention.

INTENTIONAL SELF-CARE PRACTICES

Use crystals during self-care routines, such as placing them near your bath or incorporating them into skin-care rituals, to support emotional and physical well-being. Enjoy a cup of nourishing herbal tea as part of your self-care routine, infusing it with the intention of nurturing and replenishing your energy. A tea brew may also be empowered within a grid for aura repair or beauty and mixed in within the bath for a full magickal effect.

Wind down in the evening with a calming tea crystal ritual, using herbs that support relaxation, sleep, or dream magick. Place crystals around your tea near your bedside or create a small grid in your bedroom to promote peaceful sleep and aura healing, or prophetic dreams as you unwind for the night.

By integrating tea and crystal practices into daily life, individuals can create a holistic and intentional approach to nurturing well-being, fostering mindfulness, and learning to incorporate magick into everyday mundane acts. Whether used for meditation, self-care, or clarity, the combination of tea and crystal practices provides a powerful charge for aligning with the energies within yourself.

Meditations

Tea crystal grid meditations offer a powerful and transformative practice for balancing energy, promoting emotional healing, gaining deeper spiritual insight, and tuning in to your own greater power. By incorporating tea and the intentional arrangement of crystals into a meditative practice, individuals can create a resonant and harmonious energetic framework that supports their magickal growth, personal well-being, and energetic alignment. Here are three powerful crystal grid meditations for energy alignment and healing, specifically focusing on movement, sound, and breath work.

Meditation of Movement

A meditation tea ritual within a crystal grid focusing on movement creates a beautiful blend of calming, and physical and mental discipline, fit to help align your physical and energetic bodies, promoting balance, flexibility, and tranquility. This is a great meditation to do in the morning to help awaken the day and to set goals and intentions.

SETTING UP YOUR SACRED SPACE

Choose a quiet, spacious area. Ensure you have enough room to move freely in your movement practice. Keep this space regularly cleansed. You can use rosemary, palo santo, cleansing spray, sound bowls, or even just open the windows to let in fresh air to cleanse the area energetically.

CREATE YOUR CRYSTAL GRID

Arrange four crystals in a geometric pattern on the floor in your space. Set them at each of the cardinal points (north, east, south, west). Be sure to program and activate them as you set them in place. Use crystals associated with grounding and energy flow, especially ones to set the tone for the day and fit with your intentions, like black tourmaline for protection and grounding, carnelian for vitality, and rose quartz for heart-opening. These crystals will form an empowering energy field.

PREPARE YOUR TEA STATION

Within your space, set up a small table or tray with a teapot and cup, or a cup alone, and your chosen loose-leaf tea. Choose a tea blend that will best promote renewal and clarity. Green tea is an excellent choice for the morning, with ginger and dried lemon peel.

The Ritual

BEGIN WITH TEA PREPARATION

Begin with mindful brewing. Before starting your movement practice, begin brewing your tea. As you wait for the water to boil and the tea to steep, take this moment to set an intention for your day. Whether it's seeking clarity, strength, or growth, let this intention infuse into the tea along with the herbs.

TRANSITION TO MOVEMENT

Start your movement session by standing in Mountain Pose. Stand tall at the center with your hands at your heart. Begin to focus your energy into alignment, and direct that energy towards your intentions set for the day. Be sure to synchronize your breath with your fluid movements. Inhale and bring your arms out to the sides and up to the ceiling to join your palms above your head. Lift your gaze to your thumbs and allow your shoulders to naturally extend upward. Release your breath and transition into Tree Pose and hold for three breaths. As you release on your last breath, transition into Warrior ll and hold for three breaths for each side. Continue the flow of energy by lowering yourself to Downward Dog for three breaths. Release and enter Cobra Pose, opening your chest to receive your intentions for the day. Finish with Child's Pose for three deep breaths.

After your movement practice, transition into a seated meditation position within your crystal grid. Begin sipping your tea mindfully, focusing on the sensation of warmth and the flavors. Let the act of drinking tea be a continuation of your movement practice, a physical and spiritual absorption of energy and intention.

CONCLUDING THE RITUAL

After finishing your tea, spend a few moments in silence, reflecting on your practice and the sensations within your body and mind. Close your ritual by expressing gratitude to yourself for dedicating this time to your well-being, to the earth for the tea and the crystals, and to the universe for its endless energy. Be sure to deactivate the crystals and cleanse them. Clean up mindfully.

Remember, the keys to this ritual are intention and presence. Allow yourself to fully experience each moment, from preparing the tea to sitting among the crystals, focusing on your breath. This practice can become a powerful tool for grounding and centering, offering peace and clarity amidst the busyness of life.

Meditation of Chant

When you create a meditation tea ritual within a crystal grid, focusing on a mantra and chanting technique, it offers a unique way to blend the vibrational power of crystals, the soothing nature of tea, and the transformative energy of sound. This ritual can help deepen your meditation, enhance focus, and promote a sense of inner peace and clarity. This is especially helpful midway through the day when your voice matters and it is important to check in with your inner wellness.

SETTING UP YOUR SPACE

Select a quiet area. Choose a peaceful spot where you can sit comfortably and undisturbed. Keep this space regularly cleansed. You can use rosemary, palo santo, cleansing spray, sound bowls, or even just open the windows to let in fresh air to cleanse the area energetically. This space may also be outdoors—even better to get your voice out to the universe.

CREATE YOUR CRYSTAL GRID

Arrange eight crystals in a circular pattern around your chosen meditation spot. Be sure to program and activate them as you set them in place. Consider using crystals that are known to enhance communication and spiritual connection, such as lapis lazuli, sodalite, and clear quartz. These crystals can help amplify the energy of your mantras and support throat chakra healing.

PREPARE YOUR TEA STATION

Set up a small table or tray within the space next to you with everything you need to brew your tea. Keep a selenite crystal near your teacup. Opt for a tea blend that empowers the throat chakra and promotes clarity, like oolong tea, lemon balm, fenugreek seeds, and dandelion blossoms.

The Ritual

BEGIN WITH TEA PREPARATION

Brew your tea mindfully, as you prepare your tea. Center yourself and start to focus on your breath. Let the act of brewing tea be a meditative practice. Visualize your intentions for the meditation infusing into the water along with the tea. Speak directly to the brew. You may say either your mantra or your intentions towards the rest of the day.

MANTRA SELECTION

Choose your mantra. Select a mantra that resonates with your current intentions or emotional state. For general peace and clarity, choose the mantra "Om Shanti" (peace) or "So Hum" (I am that).

PREPARE YOUR SPACE

Once your tea is ready, sit comfortably within your crystal grid. Hold your cup, feel its warmth, and take a few sips, allowing its calming energy to prepare you for meditation.

CHANTING AND MEDITATION

Begin chanting. Holding your intention in your mind, start reciting your chosen mantra out loud. Let the vibration of the chant permeate your being. Focus on the sound and feel its resonance within your body and the surrounding space, amplified by the crystal grid. Integrate with your breath. Synchronize your chanting with your breath— for example, inhale deeply and chant on the exhale. This integration helps deepen your meditation and maintain focus.

After you've finished your chanting, sit in silence for a few minutes, observing the effects of the mantra on your mind and body. Sip your tea, letting its warmth and energy settle your thoughts and emotions. Close your ritual by expressing gratitude. Thank your crystals for their energy, your tea for its healing properties, and yourself for dedicating time to your spiritual practice. Be sure to deactivate the crystals and cleanse them. Clean up mindfully. As you clean up, maintain a state of gratitude, considering this an extension of your meditation practice.

This ritual combines the grounding and energizing elements of crystals, the calming nature of tea, and the transformative power of mantra chanting to create a holistic meditation experience. By incorporating these elements, you engage multiple senses and energies, deepening your meditation and enhancing its benefits on your mind and spirit.

Meditation of Breath

Creating a meditation tea ritual within a crystal grid that is focused on breathing techniques can be a deeply soothing and releasing experience, especially in the evening when you have settled down at the end of the day and are ready to end the day. Here's a step-by-step guide to help you set up this ritual:

SETTING UP YOUR SPACE

Find a quiet spot. Choose a quiet, comfortable space where you won't be disturbed. Keep this space regularly cleansed. You can use

rosemary, palo santo, cleansing spray, sound bowls, or even just open the windows to let in fresh air to cleanse the area energetically.

SET UP YOUR CRYSTAL GRID

Arrange crystals in a basic geometric pattern on the floor or on a table where you'll be sitting. Gather four large clear quartz crystal towers and set them at each of the cardinal points (north, east, south, west) to create a balanced energy field. Be sure to program and activate them as you set them in place. You may hold crystals that aid in meditation and relaxation, such as amethyst for tranquility, clear quartz for clarity, and selenite for cleansing.

PREPARE YOUR TEA

Choose a tea blend that will best promote relaxation and release. A calming chamomile with passionflower, violet blossoms, and fresh thyme will be an excellent blend. Brew your tea mindfully. As you prepare your tea, focus and connect on each step of the process. Observe the water heating, the tea steeping, and the aroma that fills the air. Allow this process to be meditative as well. Pour your tea into a favorite and loyal cup. Choose a cup that feels special to you, enhancing the ritualistic aspect of this practice.

BEGIN YOUR MEDITATION

Sit comfortably within your crystal grid. Position yourself at the center of the grid with your tea. Sit in a comfortable position, with your back straight to promote easy breathing. Connect with your breath by closing your eyes and bringing your focus to your breathing.

Breathe in deeply through your nose for four seconds, hold for four seconds, and then exhale slowly through your mouth for four seconds. Continue to focus on your breath, noticing any areas of tension in your body and consciously relaxing them with each exhale.

After four rounds of focused breathing, slowly open your eyes and bring your teacup to your lips. Take a small sip mindfully, savoring the taste and warmth. Between sips, close your eyes again and return your focus to your breath. Let the act of drinking be part of your meditation, allowing the warmth and flavors to anchor you in the present moment. This breath-work exercise can be done for however long feels comfortable to you or you are able to do. I personally do four minutes total, but some days have been longer.

CONCLUDING THE RITUAL

Reflect on the experience. Once you finish your tea, take a few moments to reflect on the meditation and any thoughts or feelings that arose. Close the ritual. Be sure to deactivate the crystals and cleanse them. Thank yourself for taking this time for self-care. You may also want to express gratitude to the earth for the tea and the crystals that supported your meditation. Clean up mindfully. As you clean up, continue to be present. This is part of the ritual, not separate from it.

A Crystal Tea Witch's
Magickal Remedies

The intricate world of crystal grids introduces us to the captivating designs of energy and intention. As we carefully arrange crystals in sacred patterns, we create a dynamic field of energy that resonates with our deepest desires. We learn to harness the innate power of gemstones, amplifying our intentions and manifesting our aspirations with clarity and purpose. Through the art of tea magick, we can infuse intention into every aspect of our tea-making process, creating blends that align with our spiritual goals and nourish our souls. We become present in the moment, embracing the meditative qualities of tea preparation and consumption and we plant the seeds of transformation, allowing our intentions to take root and bloom within ourselves and, thus, throughout our lives.

When these two ancient practices intertwine, a profound alchemy unfolds. The transformative power of combining tea and crystal grids lies in the harmonious interplay of energies—the soothing, grounding properties of tea merge with the amplifying, clarifying energies of crystals, creating a potent catalyst for change.

The following magickal remedies allow you to infuse your daily life with the transformative energies of tea magick and crystal grids and serve as powerful tools for healing and transformation.

Astral Travel Grid Remedy

This grid remedy combines the energies of herbs, crystals, and intention to facilitate or enhance an astral travel experience. Remember, the effectiveness of such practices depends on your personal intentions, continuous practice, and the energy you put into the ritual. This remedy is especially potent when practiced between the waxing moon and the full moon.

GRID

Vesica piscis

INGREDIENTS AND TOOLS

Crystals

4 amethyst (for spiritual protection and enhancement)
1 clear quartz (for amplifying intentions and energy)
4 labradorite (for accessing the spiritual plane)

Herbs for Tea

½ teaspoon mugwort
1 tablespoon spearmint
½ teaspoon angelica root
1 star anise

A teapot or cup
A tea warmer or tall trivet
A small cloth or space

PREPARATION

Start by cleansing your space and items (crystals, teapot/cup, and herbs) using your preferred method. Set your intention and program each crystal, instructing them on their purpose for the grid. Prepare your tea. Mindfully boil your water and pour it over your blend. Let it steep for 5 to 10 minutes. As it steeps, meditate on your intention and what you wish to accomplish or discover during your astral travel.

Create your crystal grid. While your tea is steeping, begin setting up your vesica piscis grid. Start with placing your tea warmer or tall trivet at the center of the cloth or space. Lay out the amethyst at the bottom circle, aligning them around the circle and tea warmer/ trivet, making sure it's tidy. Lay the labradorite carefully around the top circle. Place the clear quartz in the center within the warmer/ trivet, stating your intentions once more. Once your grid is set up, use a wand or your finger to connect each crystal, starting from the bottom circle moving clockwise, envisioning each crystal lighting up and connecting with the next. Visualize the grid activating and a protective, enhancing energy rising up into the tea.

Strain and then slowly drink your tea, allowing yourself to relax and open up to the experience. Visualize your astral body preparing to travel. After drinking your tea, sit comfortably or lie down in a safe, quiet space. Close your eyes, relax, and focus on your intention. Allow yourself to drift into a meditative state, open to the experiences of astral travel.

Remember, patience and practice are key. Your experience can vary from subtle energetic shifts to profound spiritual journeys. Trust the process and your own intuition.

Aura Repair Grid Remedy

This grid remedy is a thoughtful way to support and mend your energetic field. This ritual is intended to heal and strengthen your aura, especially when you have found yourself feeling moody, tired, lifeless, or drained. It is most ideal to do this remedy when the moon is new and you can prepare a bath right after.

GRID

Lemniscate (figure eight)

INGREDIENTS AND TOOLS

Crystals

5 black tourmaline (for protection and grounding)
1 selenite plate (for cleansing and clearing negative energy)
5 rose quartz (for love and healing)

Herbs for Tea

1 teaspoon nettle
1 teaspoon calendula
½ teaspoon rose hips
½ teaspoon chamomile

A small teapot or cup
A bath rug or bath tray

PREPARATION

Begin by cleansing your space and items (crystals, teapot/cup, and herbs) using your preferred method. Now set your intention: program your crystals with your intention for aura repair. Focus on healing, protection, and rejuvenation.

Prepare your tea. Boil water and pour it over your blend. Let it steep for about 10 minutes. While it steeps, focus on your intention to heal and protect your aura.

Create your crystal grid. As your tea is steeping, set up your crystal grid on your bath rug or bath tray, preferably within your bathroom. Place the selenite plate at the center to signify purity and cleansing. Arrange the black tourmaline on the lower loop for grounding and protection. Lay the rose quartz on the upper loop for healing and energizing light. Place your small teapot or cup upon the selenite plate.

Activate your grid. With a wand or your finger, draw an invisible line connecting each crystal, starting from the selenite, moving clockwise to each of the crystals. As you do this, visualize a bright, protective light activating the grid and enveloping your tea, enhancing its healing properties.

Gently sip your tea, allowing its warmth and the energy of the grid to fill and repair your aura. Visualize any tears or weaknesses in your aura being sealed with light and love. After drinking your tea,

prepare a bath and sit or lie down within the cleansing waters, with your crystal grid nearby. Close your eyes and meditate, visualizing your aura as a luminous field around you, glowing brighter and becoming whole with each breath.

Once you feel the process is complete, give thanks to the herbs, crystals, and your higher self or any spiritual guides for their support in repairing your aura. Gently rise from the bath and air dry. Dismantle the grid, cleansing and storing the crystals and disposing of the tea leaves in a respectful manner. Engaging regularly with this ritual can help maintain a resilient and vibrant aura, supporting overall well-being and spiritual health.

Binding Grid Remedy

This grid remedy focuses on the intention to bind or hold something in place, whether it's to prevent harm, stop gossip, end a bad habit, or stabilize a situation. This spell combines the energies of specific crystals and herbs with the power of intention to create a protective or stabilizing effect. It's important to approach this with a clear, ethical intent, focusing on protection rather than manipulation or harm.

GRID

Pentagram

INGREDIENTS AND TOOLS

Crystals

2 black obsidian (for protection and grounding)
2 hematite (for grounding and boundary-setting)

1 tiger's eye (for protection and strength)
1 smoky quartz (for neutralizing negative energy)

Herbs for Tea

1 strong black tea bag
1 cinnamon stick
Cloves

A cup and saucer
A small black cloth
Black pen

PREPARATION

Use your preferred method to cleanse your space, crystals, teacup, and herbs. Set your intention. Write down either a word or symbol—your specific intention for the binding—on the tea tag. Be precise and focus on protection, stabilization, or halting negative actions. Place this tea bag within your teacup. Place your cup upon the saucer at the center of your grid or space where you'll be setting up. Create your crystal grid. You will arrange your crystals around the outside of your saucer. Place the tiger's eye at the top point. Follow the line down to place a black obsidian at the bottom left. Place a hematite up and across. Place the second hematite straight across. Place the second black obsidian down at the remaining bottom right point. Place the smoky quartz in the center of your teacup, on top of the tea bag to absorb and neutralize negativity. Arrange the whole cloves around your teacup, within the saucer.

Activate your grid with the cinnamon stick as your wand: tapping to connect each crystal starting from the top of the pentagram and back again. Focus upon the smoky quartz, envisioning a protective barrier forming. Imagine each connection emitting light, binding the grid and your tea with your intention.

Prepare your tea. Mindfully boil water. When ready, remove the smoky quartz from the cup, still keeping within range of the grid while you pour the boiled water over the black tea. Add your cinnamon stick, and let it steep for 5 to 10 minutes while you focus on your intention. Imagine the tea absorbing your intention, becoming a potent brew for protection and binding.

As you drink your tea and hold on to the smoky quartz, visualize it reinforcing your aura, making it impenetrable to the negativity or actions you wish to bind. With each sip, strengthen your resolve and your intention. After drinking your tea, meditate, and repeat an affirmation that aligns with your intention, such as "I am protected and shielded from harm. My boundaries are respected and upheld."

Give thanks to the herbs, crystals, and any higher powers you believe in for their protection and assistance. When you feel the work is done, dismantle the grid, cleanse, and store the crystals. When disposing of the tea bag, collect and wrap the string tightly around the bag. Seal it in a jar and hide it in a dark place where it will never be disturbed.

Courage Grid Remedy

This grid remedy involves invoking the power of crystals and herbs to enhance your inner strength, bravery, and resolve. This spell is designed to help you face challenges, overcome fears, and step into your power with confidence.

GRID

Hexagram

INGREDIENTS AND TOOLS

Crystals

3 carnelian (for courage and vitality)
1 tiger's eye (for courage, protection, and power)
3 clear quartz (to amplify the energies and intention)

Herbs for Tea

1 teaspoon rooibos
1 pinch of powdered cinnamon
1 pinch of powdered ginger
1 teaspoon saffron

A teapot or cup
A small cloth

PREPARATION

Begin by cleansing your area, crystals, teapot/cup, and herbs. You can use smoke, sound cleansing, or any method you prefer to remove negative energy and create a sacred space. Set your intention and program the crystals with the aspects of your life where you seek

courage. Be as specific as possible. This could be courage in facing a particular situation, making a decision, or asserting yourself.

Create your crystal grid. Place the three clear quartz upon the first triangle pointing up. Join and activate these points. Arrange the three carnelian in the overlocking triangle over the top of the first pointing down. Join and activate these points with the first crystal you laid. Have your herbal blend within a cup and place this at the center of the grid. Place your cleansed tiger's eye upon the herbs. Ensure each crystal's placement is intentional and focused on enhancing courage. Activate your center crystal. As you do this, imagine a fiery light linking the crystals, creating a network of energy that pulsates with strength and courage that specifically transfers to the herbal blend.

Mindfully boil your water. Take your cup from the grid, remove the tiger's eye, and place it back within the grid. Brew your tea and allow it to steep for about 10 minutes while you focus on your intention, visualizing yourself facing your challenges with strength and confidence. Now sip your tea slowly, internalizing its warmth and energy. Visualize the fiery energy from the tea merging with your own, bolstering your courage and preparing you to face whatever comes your way with a brave heart. After drinking your tea, sit or lie down near your crystal grid. Close your eyes and meditate on your intention. Visualize yourself overcoming fears and stepping into your power with confidence. Feel the support of the crystals and the energy of the tea infusing you with courage.

Once you feel the energy work is complete, express gratitude to the crystals, the herbs, and any higher powers you called upon. Carefully dismantle your grid, cleanse and store the crystals. Dispose of the tea leaves in a way that feels respectful and in alignment with your intentions.

Divination Grid Remedy

This grid harnesses the intuitive energies of crystals and the insightful properties of herbs to enhance your divinatory practices, whether you're working with tarot cards, runes, scrying, or any other form of divination. This spell is designed to open your third eye, sharpen your intuition, and connect you to higher wisdom. Can be done when needed, but especially potent during the new or full moon.

GRID

Square

INGREDIENTS AND TOOLS

Crystals

4 labradorite (for awakening mystical and magickal abilities and enhancing psychic powers)

Herbs for Tea

1 pinch mugwort

1 tablespoon dandelion root

1 tablespoon hibiscus

1 tablespoon dried orange peel

1 tablespoon dried fig

Bowl

A teapot or cup

A purple cloth

Divination tool

PREPARATION

Using your preferred method (such as smudging with incense, sound cleansing, or cleansing spray), cleanse your area, crystals, teapot/cup, and herbs of any negative or stagnant energies.

Set your intention. Prepare your tea. Blend your tea within the bowl and place it at the center of the purple cloth. Boil your water mindfully, then set your teapot and cup near the grid space. Create your crystal grid, and program your crystals with your intentions. Arrange your first labradorite in the top left corner of the square. Lay your second in the corner to the right of the first. Lay your third below that in the next corner. Lay your final one in the last corner. Activate your grid with a wand or your finger, connecting each crystal by drawing invisible lines between them. As you do this, envision a luminous web of energy connecting the crystals, charging your tea blend with the purpose of opening your intuitive channels, creating an energetic boundary that enhances psychic perception and protects your divinatory space.

Take a tablespoon of tea blend from the bowl and place into your teapot. Pour your hot water mindfully, and let it steep for about 10 minutes. As it steeps, contemplate your intention, and visualize the tea drawing down cosmic or intuitive insights into your cup. Take a handful of the tea blend and create a circle within the square grid.

Sip your tea, allowing its insightful energies to fill you. Visualize it as a liquid light, illuminating your mind and opening your third eye, preparing you for the divination work ahead. Now that your intuitive senses are heightened, proceed with your divination practice. Keep your intention or question in mind as you shuffle your tarot cards, cast your runes, or gaze into your crystal ball. Do your practice within the grid and circle of herbs.

After your divination session, meditate on the insights received, reflecting on how the messages resonate with your intuition. Consider any actions you might take moving forward. Express gratitude to the herbs, crystals, and any higher powers or guides for their assistance. Carefully dismantle your grid; cleanse and store your crystals. Compost the tea leaves, returning them to the earth with thanks. You may save the rest of the tea blend to use for future divination remedies. Regularly integrating this ritual into your spiritual work can help maintain a clear and open channel for receiving guidance and wisdom.

Friendship Grid Remedy

Creating this grid remedy is a beautiful way to enhance existing friendships, attract new friends, or even heal misunderstandings within relationships. This spell combines the loving energies of crystals and the bonding power of herbs to foster understanding, harmony, and mutual respect in friendships.

GRID

Vesica piscis

INGREDIENTS AND TOOLS

Crystals

1 rose quartz (for unconditional love and friendship)
8 green aventurine (for emotional healing and harmony)
8 clear quartz (to amplify the energies and intentions)

Herbs for Tea

1 teaspoon oolong tea

1 teaspoon hibiscus

1 teaspoon jasmine

1 sprig of fresh mint

A teapot or cup

Tea warmer or tall trivet

A pink cloth

PREPARATION

Begin by cleansing your area, crystals, teapot or cup, and herbs. You can use methods like smudging with incense, sound cleansing, or visualization to purify your space from any negative energies. Focus on your intentions for your friendships, be they strengthening existing bonds, healing misunderstandings, or attracting new, meaningful connections. Place these intentions into your grid or space where you'll be setting up.

Prepare your tea mindfully as you heat your water to 195 degrees and pour it over your tea blend. Let it steep for about 3 to 5 minutes. While it steeps, focus on your intentions for your friendships, visualizing them flourishing and filled with joy and understanding.

Create your crystal grid by arranging the green aventurines on the left-hand circle first. Outline the right-hand circle (overlapping) with the clear quartz. If this grid is for creating friendships, you may place jasmine or hibiscus flowers in between the crystals. If this grid is for healing or mending relationships, use fresh mint between the crystals. Place the tea warmer or tall trivet at the center. Place the

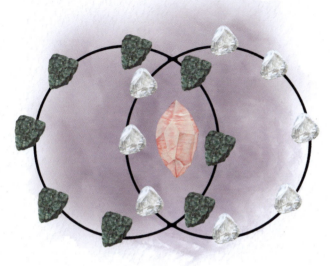

rose quartz at the center of this tea warmer or trivet as a symbol of the heart of your friendships. With each crystal's placement, focus on enhancing the qualities you wish to bring into your friendships. Place your brewed tea upon the warmer/trivet. Activate your grid by using a wand, mind, or your finger; draw energetic lines connecting each crystal, starting from the rose quartz and moving outward. As you do this, envision a warm, loving light linking the crystals, creating a network of energy that radiates friendship and understanding, and send this energy to your brew.

When ready, sip your tea. Imagine its warmth and flavor embodying the qualities of the friendships you desire. Visualize it nourishing your heart and soul, preparing you to give and receive friendship with open arms. After finishing your tea, spend some time meditating near your crystal grid. Visualize your current and future friendships blossoming, filled with laughter, support, and mutual respect. Imagine any misunderstandings being healed and replaced with understanding and forgiveness. Once you feel the work is complete, express gratitude for the support of the crystals, herbs, and any higher powers you believe in. Carefully dismantle your grid, cleanse and store the crystals. Dispose of the tea leaves in a respectful manner, perhaps drying them and placing them in a small pink or white bag.

By regularly engaging with this remedy, you can maintain a loving and supportive energy around your friendships, encouraging them to grow and thrive in harmony and mutual respect.

Happiness Grid Remedy

This remedy is a wonderful way to attract joy, uplift your spirits, and infuse your life with happiness. This spell combines the sunny energy of crystals and the uplifting properties of herbs to create a beacon of joy in your life. Especially favored when done between the waxing and full moon.

GRID

Sunburst

INGREDIENTS AND TOOLS

Crystals
8 citrine (for happiness and joy)
8 sunstone (for positivity and good luck)

Herbs for Tea
1 teaspoon red clover

1 teaspoon lavender
¼ teaspoon marjoram
Honey

9 sprigs fresh thyme
1 dried lemon slice
A cup
A yellow or white cloth

PREPARATION

Begin by cleansing your area, crystals, cup, and herbs. You can use smudging with incense, sound cleansing, or cleansing spray to clear away any negative energies and create a sacred, positive space. Set your intention. Program your crystals and herbs for bringing happiness into your life. Be specific about the areas you wish to improve or the general feeling of joy you want to cultivate.

Prepare your tea mindfully within your cup, adding one fresh sprig of thyme. Boil water and pour it over the blend, letting it steep for about 10 minutes. While it steeps, focus on your intentions for happiness, visualizing your life filled with laughter, joy, and contentment.

Create your crystal grid by placing the dried lemon slice at the center of your cloth as a symbol of the essence of happiness. Use your intuition to surround it with citrine in a sunburst shape. Then lay out the sunstones on the outer circle around the citrines. Take the eight remaining sprigs of fresh thyme and place them in a straight line bursting outward in a pattern that feels joyful and uplifting to you, with each placement focusing on amplifying happiness and positive

energy. Place your cup of tea over the dried lemon slice.

Activate your grid by using a wand, mind, or your finger. Draw energetic lines connecting each crystal, starting from the lemon slice and moving outward. As you do this, envision a bright, cheerful light linking the crystals and herbs, creating a network of energy that radiates happiness and joy. As you sip your tea, imagine its warmth and flavor embodying the qualities of happiness and joy you seek. Visualize the tea's energy filling you from within, spreading warmth and happiness throughout your body and soul.

After finishing your tea, spend some time meditating near your crystal grid. Visualize yourself experiencing moments of pure joy, laughter, and contentment in various aspects of your life. See yourself surrounded by positive energy and people who contribute to your happiness. Once you feel the work is complete, express gratitude for the support of the crystals, herbs, and any higher powers you believe in. Carefully dismantle your grid, cleanse and store the crystals. Or, if you wish for this grid to continue its effects, you may leave it activated between phases. Be sure to continuously cleanse and replenish.

By regularly engaging with this remedy, you can create a positive, joyful energy in your life and environment that attracts happiness and contentment. Remember, happiness is a journey, not a destination, and this spell can be a beautiful part of that journey.

Healing Grid Remedy

This remedy combines the nurturing energies of crystals and the restorative properties of herbs to foster physical, emotional, or spiritual healing. This spell is designed to support your healing journey, complementing traditional healing methods with a touch of holistic and energetic healing. It is recommended to do this remedy bimonthly, preferably during the new moons. This will help renew the body's ability to heal itself.

GRID

Lemniscate

INGREDIENTS AND TOOLS

Crystals

1 green aventurine (for physical healing and well-being)

1 amethyst (for spiritual healing and protection)

1 selenite (to amplify the energies and intentions)

Herbs for Tea

1 teaspoon echinacea

1 teaspoon peppermint

1 teaspoon lavender

1 teaspoon chamomile

A cup

A blue cloth

With incense smoke, sound cleansing, visualization, or cleansing spray, cleanse your area, crystals, cup, and herbs of any negative or stagnant energies, setting a pure and healing atmosphere. Set your intentions for healing, whether it's for physical health, emotional balance, spiritual growth, or a combination. Program this intention into your crystals, herbs, and the space where you'll be setting up.

Prepare your tea mindfully while boiling your water. Pour it over your blend and let steep for about 10 minutes. During this time, focus on your healing intentions, envisioning the tea imbued with restorative and calming energies.

Create your crystal grid: you will be placing yourself at the center where you will be lying down. Place the clear quartz in the spot beneath your where feet will lie; place the selenite crystal above where your head will be. Lastly, hold the green aventurine at the center of your body along with your cup of tea, as a symbol of the heart of your healing process. Focus on the qualities of healing you wish to bring into your life. Activate your grid by using your mind to draw energetic lines connecting each crystal. As you do this, envision a soothing, healing light linking the crystals, creating a network of energy focused on healing and well-being. Now sit up to sip your tea, letting its healing energy wash over you. Visualize the tea as a potion of health, soothing any ailments, calming the mind, and restoring your spirit.

After finishing your tea, lie back down and meditate within your crystal grid. Visualize the healing energies from the grid and the tea working together, focusing on the areas you wish to heal. See yourself healthy, vibrant, and whole. Remain between 5 and 15 minutes. If you become aware of any energy that needs to be released from your body, send it down to the crystal at your feet to be released and transformed. Once you feel the work is complete, express gratitude to the crystals, herbs, and any higher powers or guides for their support in your healing journey. Carefully dismantle your grid, cleanse and store the crystals.

By regularly practicing this remedy, you can support your journey to health and well-being, creating a harmonious balance between body, mind, and spirit. Remember, healing is a process, and this ritual can be a comforting and empowering part of that process. This grid may also be laid beneath the bed for continued healing.

Hex-Breaker Grid Remedy

This remedy is a potent way to dispel negative energy, break curses or hexes, and protect yourself from further negativity. This spell combines the protective energies of crystals with the cleansing properties of herbs to create a powerful shield of positivity. This remedy can be done immediately, but it is especially potent between the waning and new moon.

GRID

Pentagram

INGREDIENTS AND TOOLS

Crystals
8 black tourmaline (for protection and grounding)
1 smoky quartz (for negativity absorption and detoxification)
5 labradorite (for deflecting unwanted energies)

Herbs for Tea

1 teaspoon Earl Grey black tea

½ teaspoon vetiver

1 teaspoon chamomile

A teapot and cup

A black cloth

Tea warmer or tall trivet

PREPARATION

Cleanse your space and items using incense, sound cleansing, spray cleansing, or visualization; this will clear your space, crystals, teapot, cup, and herbs of any negative or stagnant energies, setting a protective and pure atmosphere. Set your intention by programming your crystals and herbs with your intention for breaking any hexes or curses, or for shielding yourself from negativity. Be specific and focused.

Prepare your tea within the teapot and manfully boil moon water and pour it over the tea blend. Let it steep for about 4 to 5 minutes. During this time, focus on your intention, visualizing yourself being freed from any negative influences and surrounded by a protective light.

Create your crystal grid. Place the tea warmer/trivet at the center of your cloth. Arrange the five labradorite crystals as a pentagram. Outside the pentagram, arrange the black tourmaline in a circle. Place the smoky quartz within the tea warmer/trivet in the center as a symbol of your core, absorbing negativity and detoxifying. Envision the grid becoming protective and reinforcing, each crystal working to break hexes and shielding you. Activate your grid, using a wand, mind, or your finger. Draw energetic lines connecting each crystal. As you do this, envision a powerful, protective barrier being formed, encapsulating you in a bubble of positive energy that repels negativity, and direct this energy within your tea brew.

Sip your tea, visualizing its cleansing properties washing away any hexes, curses, or negativity from your body and spirit. Imagine the tea infusing you with strength and a protective shield against further attacks. After finishing your tea, meditate near your crystal grid. Picture the combined energies of the crystals and the tea working together to fortify your protective barrier. Visualize any hexes or curses dissolving and see yourself shining with a brilliant, protective light.

Once you feel the work is complete, express gratitude to the crystals, herbs, and any guides or higher powers you believe in for their protection and support. Carefully dismantle your grid, cleanse and store the crystals. Dispose of the tea leaves in a respectful manner, perhaps offering them to the earth far away from your home, as a gesture of release and gratitude.

This grid can be a powerful way to cleanse yourself of negativity and protect against future magickal attacks. Remember, the strength of your intention and belief in the ritual's efficacy are key to its success. This spell can be repeated as needed, especially during times when you feel particularly vulnerable to negative energies. This grid may also be kept activated until the energy has been reinforced. Be sure to cleanse and replenish it until it is ready to be dismantled.

Love Grid Remedy

This remedy is a magickal way to attract love, enhance existing relationships, or cultivate self-love and inner harmony. This spell combines the gentle energies of crystals with the heart-opening properties of herbs, setting the stage for love to enter or flourish in your life. May be either enjoyed alone or shared with a potential partner. Powerful when performed on a Friday during the waxing moon. Follow this guide to perform this enchanting ritual.

GRID

Vesica piscis

INGREDIENTS AND TOOLS

Crystals

1 rose quartz (for unconditional love and heart healing)

8 rhodonite (for emotional balance and clearing away wounds)

8 clear quartz (to amplify the energies and intentions)

Herbs for Tea

1 teaspoon rose petals

1 teaspoon hibiscus

1 teaspoon yarrow

1 tablespoon dried strawberries

1 teaspoon sugar

A cup or teapot

Tea warmer/tall trivet

A pink cloth

Paper and pen

PREPARATION

Begin by cleansing your space, crystals, teapot or cup, and herbs of any negative or stagnant energies. Set your intentions by writing down your intention focused on love. It could relate to attracting new love, enhancing self-love, or strengthening a current relationship. Place this intention under the center of your grid or space where you'll be setting up. Place the tea warmer/trivet over this paper.

Prepare your tea. Boil water and pour it over your blend. Let it steep for about 10 minutes. As it's steeping, focus on your love intentions, visualizing your life filled with the love you wish to attract or enhance. Place your teapot or cup upon your tea warmer/trivet.

Create your crystal grid by placing the rose quartz inside your tea warmer/trivet at the center of your cloth or designated space as a symbol of your heart's center, radiating unconditional love. Arrange the top loop with rhodonite and the bottom loop, overlapping, with the clear quartz, focusing on various aspects of love and emotional well-being. Activate your grid by using either a wand, mind, or your finger. Draw energetic lines connecting each crystal, starting from the rose quartz and moving outward. As you do this, envision a warm, loving light connecting the crystals, creating a powerful matrix of energy centered on attracting or enhancing love. Visualize and draw this energy towards your tea brew.

Sip your tea, imagining its loving properties infusing your body and spirit, opening your heart to give and receive love. Visualize the tea as a liquid manifestation of your intentions for love. After finishing your tea, meditate near your crystal grid. Hover your hands over the grid and absorb the energy within your hands. Caress your face, skin, and heart, and visualize the combined energies of the crystals and the

tea working together to attract love into your life or enhance the love you already share. Picture yourself surrounded by warmth, affection, and harmony.

Once you feel the work is complete, express gratitude to the crystals, herbs, and any guides or higher powers you believe in for their support in your journey toward love. Carefully dismantle your grid, cleanse and store the crystals. This grid may also be kept activated until the love you seek enters your life. Be sure to continue cleansing and replenishing it.

Engaging with this remedy can be a powerful way to set your intentions for love into motion. Remember, the strength of your intention and belief in the ritual's efficacy are key to its success. This spell can be repeated as needed, whenever you feel called to reaffirm your commitment to love.

Luck Grid Remedy

This remedy is a delightful way to attract good fortune, enhance opportunities, and open pathways to success. This spell intertwines the prosperous energies of crystals with the fortifying properties of herbs, crafting a potent catalyst for luck. Create this grid at the start of the waxing moon to invite luck into your life and keep it activated till the full moon.

GRID

Spiral

Crystals

10 citrine (for prosperity and success)

10 tiger's eye (for courage and luck)

Herbs for Tea

1 tablespoon linden flowers

Dash ground allspice

Dash ground nutmeg

Dash ground cinnamon

1 tablespoon dried orange peel

1 teaspoon black tea

1 star anise

A white cup

An orange cloth or a slate base

A muslin bag

PREPARATION

Cleanse your space and items: smudge with incense, sound cleansing, cleansing spray, or visualization to rid your space, crystals, cup, muslin bag, and herbs of any negative or stagnant energies. Set your intention and program your crystals and herbs toward attracting general good fortune, success in a specific endeavor, or opening pathways for opportunities.

Prepare and blend your tea. Secure this tea in your muslin bag and place in your cup. Mindfully boil water and keep it near where you will set up your grid.

Create your crystal grid by first placing your cup with the tea at the center of your cloth or slate base. Lay a spiral of alternated crystals of citrine and tiger's eye, pointing down and inward, until you reach the teacup. This creates a space that feels dynamic and supportive; be sure to focus on various aspects of luck and success as you lay your crystals. Activate your grid using a wand, your mind, or your finger, drawing energetic lines connecting each crystal, starting from the tea and moving outward. As you do this, envision a bright, golden light connecting the crystals, creating a powerful matrix of energy centered on attracting luck. Pour your hot water over your tea and let it steep for about 10 minutes. During this time, focus on your intentions, visualizing your life filled with the luck and opportunities you wish to attract.

Drink your tea and imagine its prosperous properties infusing your body and spirit, opening you to receive luck. Visualize the tea as a liquid manifestation of your intentions for good fortune. After finishing your tea, meditate near your crystal grid. Visualize the combined energies of the crystals and the tea working together to attract luck into your life. Picture yourself surrounded by opportunities and success, effortlessly navigating toward your goals. Once you feel the work is complete, express gratitude to the crystals, herbs, and any guides. Carefully dismantle your grid and store the crystals. Respectfully dispose of the tea leaves, perhaps by offering them to the earth; however, dry and save the star anise and use it as a charm for continued luck.

Mental Clarity Grid Remedy

This remedy is a powerful ritual designed to enhance focus, clear mental fog, and boost cognitive abilities. This spell combines the clarifying energies of crystals with the cognition-supporting properties of certain herbs, making it a potent tool for anyone seeking to improve concentration, memory, or decision-making. This remedy can be a powerful aid in times of study, when making important decisions, or whenever you seek to enhance your cognitive abilities.

GRID

Extended square

INGREDIENTS AND TOOLS

Crystals

4 fluorite (for clarity and decision-making)
4 sodalite (for logic and rational thinking)

Herbs for Tea

1 teaspoon green tea
1 teaspoon mint
1 teaspoon lemon verbena
1 sprig fresh rosemary
Slice of lemon
Honey

A teapot or green cup
A yellow cloth

Begin by cleansing your space, crystals, teapot or cup, and herbs from any negative or stagnant energies. You may use cinnamon and ginger incense, sound cleansing with a bell or singing bowl, or visualization techniques. Set your intentions and program your crystals and herbs, focused on mental clarity. Whether it's to enhance focus, improve memory, or aid in decision-making, be clear about what you seek to achieve.

Prepare your tea and blend in your teapot. Mindfully heat your water to 175 degrees and set it near your grid space. Create your crystal grid by placing the four fluorite crystals on the corners of the inner square, symbolizing mental clarity and decision-making. Place the four sodalite crystals on the corners of the outer square, focusing on the various aspects of mental clarity you wish to enhance. Lastly, place your teapot in the center of the grid. Activate your grid by using a wand, mind, or your finger, drawing energetic lines connecting each crystal. As you do this, envision a bright light connecting the crystals, creating a powerful matrix of energy centered on enhancing cognitive abilities. Then, with intention, pour the hot water over your tea, and allow it to steep for about 1 to 3 minutes. As it steeps, focus on your intentions, visualizing yourself achieving remarkable mental clarity and cognitive improvements.

Sip your tea, imagining it acting as a liquid manifestation of your intentions for cognitive improvement and infusing your body and spirit, promoting mental alertness and clarity. After finishing your tea, spend time meditating near your crystal grid. Visualize the combined energies of the crystals and the tea working together to clear any mental fog and enhance your cognitive abilities. Picture yourself achieving your goals with unparalleled focus and clarity.

Keep the grid activated until your work is complete. Express gratitude, carefully dismantle your grid, and cleanse and store the crystals. Repeat as needed, especially during times of mental strain or when embarking on projects that require significant mental effort.

Peace Grid Remedy

This remedy can be a serene and powerful ritual to invite tranquility, reduce stress, and harmonize energies within your environment, especially between family members or couples, or within yourself. This ritual combines the calming energies of crystals with the soothing properties of specific herbs to craft a sanctum of peace.

GRID

Triangle

INGREDIENTS AND TOOLS

Crystals
3 blue lace agate (for calming and soothing energies)
1 selenite plate (for cleansing and purifying)

Herbs for Tea
1 teaspoon passionflower
1 teaspoon violet blossoms
2 to 3 sprigs fresh thyme
Honey

A blue teapot and cup
A small white cloth

Begin by cleansing your space, crystals, teapot or cup, and herbs of any negative or stagnant energies. This can be done through smudging with lavender, sound cleansing, cleansing spray, or visualization. Set your intention and program your crystals and herbs towards peace. Be specific about the kind of tranquility you seek—whether it's inner peace, harmony in relationships, or a calm environment.

Prepare and mindfully blend your tea within your blue teapot. Boil water and pour over your blend. Allow it to steep for about 10 minutes. As it steeps, focus on your intentions, visualizing your life or environment imbued with a profound sense of peace and serenity. Create your crystal grid by placing the three blue lace agate crystals at each corner of the triangle, symbolizing peace and tranquility. Place

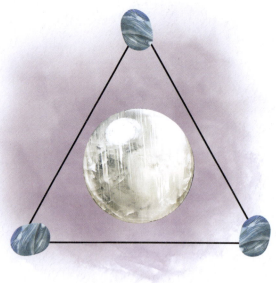

the selenite plate in the center and arrange the small white cloth upon it. Place the teapot on top of this.

Activate your grid using a wand, your mind, or your finger, drawing energetic lines connecting each crystal. As you do this, envision a soft, soothing light connecting the crystals, creating a powerful hum of energy centered on cultivating peace. Focus this energy toward your tea and space. Pour tea for yourself and for anyone else in need, imagining its calming properties infusing your body and spirit, promoting a deep sense of relaxation and peace. Visualize the tea manifesting your intentions for tranquility. After finishing your tea, allow the combined energies of the tea and crystals working together to create a sanctuary of peace around you and your space. Say a prayer for yourself or for your environment to be filled with calm, harmonious energy.

You may keep the grid activated until you and the environment feel fulfilled with peace. Carefully dismantle your grid, cleanse and store the crystals. This spell can be a powerful tool in times of turmoil or stress, or when seeking to create a sanctuary of tranquility either within yourself or in your living space. Repeat as needed, especially during challenging times or when you feel the need to realign with peace and serenity.

Prophetic Dreams Grid Remedy

Creating this remedy can be a mystical and enriching ritual for those seeking to enhance their dreamwork, intuition, and connection to the subconscious or spiritual realms. This spell combines the intuitive energies of crystals with the dream-promoting properties of specific herbs to craft an environment conducive to receiving prophetic dreams. This is best done when a full moon is at its peak.

GRID
Diamond (square)

INGREDIENTS AND TOOLS

Crystals
2 moonstone (for connecting with the subconscious and promoting prophetic dreams)
2 labradorite (for magickal transformation and accessing the Akashic records)

Herbs for Tea
1 teaspoon elderflowers
1 teaspoon passionflower
1 teaspoon thyme
1 teaspoon valerian root
1 teaspoon lavender

A glass teapot
A glass cup
A purple cloth

PREPARATION

Begin by cleansing your space, crystals, teapot or cup, and herbs from any negative or stagnant energies. This can be achieved through smudging with rosemary, sound cleansing with a bell, cleansing spray, or visualization techniques. For sleeping, you may have a humidifier on, using jasmine or lavender essential oil. Set your intention by programming your crystals and tea toward prophetic dreams. Focus on whether you're seeking guidance, answers to specific questions, or deeper spiritual insights; be clear about your purpose.

Blend and mindfully prepare your tea in the glass teapot. Boil moon water and pour it over the tea blend. Allow it to steep for about 10 minutes. As it steeps, focus on your intentions, visualizing yourself receiving clear and insightful dreams that offer guidance or answers. Create your crystal grid, preferably beside your bedside, by placing the glass teacup at the center of your cloth. Place the first moonstone at the top point of the diamond, and the second at the bottom point. Place one labradorite on the left point of the diamond, and the second across at the right point. Focus on connecting with the subconscious and promoting prophetic dreams. Activate your grid using a wand, mind, or your finger, drawing energetic lines connecting each crystal. As you do this, envision a luminous, ethereal light connecting the crystals, creating powerful energy centered on prophetic dreamwork. Focus this energy to infuse your brew.

Drink your tea and imagine its dream-promoting properties infusing your body and spirit, preparing you for insightful dreams. Meditate beside your crystal grid. Visualize the combined energies of the crystals and the tea working together to open your mind to

receiving prophetic dreams. Picture yourself peacefully falling asleep and receiving clear, insightful messages in your dreams.

Prepare for bed as usual, keeping your intentions in mind. Leave the grid activated overnight. In the morning, carefully dismantle your grid, cleanse and store the crystals. Respectfully dispose of the tea leaves. This spell can be a powerful practice for those looking to deepen their dreamwork practice, enhance intuition, or seek guidance through dreams. Repeat as desired, especially when seeking guidance, or when you feel particularly drawn to explore the world of dreams.

Prosperity Grid Remedy

This remedy is an engaging and powerful ritual aimed at attracting abundance, wealth, and success into your life. By combining the transformative energies of crystals with the prosperity-enhancing properties of specific herbs, you can create a potent focal point for manifesting financial stability and abundance. This grid is best done on a Thursday or during new moons.

GRID

Pentagram

INGREDIENTS AND TOOLS

Crystals

8 citrine (for abundance and success)

5 green aventurine (for luck and prosperity)

1 pyrite (for wealth and good fortune)

Herbs for Tea

1 teaspoon mullein

1 teaspoon vetiver

1 teaspoon mint

1 teaspoon lemon balm

Honey

A teapot or cup

Tea warmer or tall trivet

A green cloth

PREPARATION

Begin by cleansing your space, crystals, teapot or cup, and herbs of any negative or stagnant energies. This can be achieved through smudging with benzoin and basil, sound cleansing, cleansing spray, or visualization techniques. Set your intentions and program your crystals and tea focused on prosperity. Be specific about the type of abundance you seek—be it financial wealth, success in endeavors, or general prosperity in all aspects of your life. Burn any abundance-drawing incense or even burn the above tea recipe over charcoal.

Prepare and blend your tea within your teapot. Create your crystal grid by placing your tea warmer/trivet at the center of your cloth. Place the first green aventurine at the top point of the pentagram, then at the bottom left, up and across, directly across, and at

133

the remaining bottom point. Use the citrine to form an outer circle around the pentagram. Place the pyrite within the tea warmer/trivet, focusing on attracting wealth, prosperity, and success. Set your teapot upon the tea warmer/trivet.

Activate your grid using a wand, your mind, or your finger, connecting each crystal. As you do this, envision a vibrant, golden light connecting the crystals, creating powerful energy centered on prosperity. Boil new-moon water and pour it mindfully over your tea blend, envisioning the prosperous energy infusing the brew. Allow it to steep for about 10 minutes. As it steeps, focus on your intentions, visualizing your life filled with the prosperity and abundance you desire.

Sip your tea while imagining its prosperity-attracting properties infusing your body and spirit, preparing you to receive abundance. Visualize your intentions for financial success and prosperity flowing into reality. After finishing your tea, spend time meditating near your crystal grid, fully visualizing the opportunities, wealth, and success coming into your life. Picture yourself achieving this. When finished with your tea, dismantle your grid, cleanse and store the crystals. You may dry the tea blend and scatter across the perimeters of your home and space to continue attracting abundance. This grid may also be kept activated until it has fulfilled its work. Simply remember to cleanse and replenish it. Repeat as desired, especially during financial planning, when embarking on new business ventures, or when you feel the need to boost your financial energy.

Psychic Protection Grid Remedy

This remedy is a powerful ritual designed to shield your energy and provide spiritual protection. This spell combines the protective energies of crystals with the shielding properties of specific herbs to create a potent focus for safeguarding your psychic space. This grid is best done between the waning and new moon.

GRID

Square (with inner diamond)

INGREDIENTS AND TOOLS

Crystals

4 black tourmaline (for grounding and protection against negative energy)

4 smoky quartz (for emotional and psychic protection)

1 amethyst (for spiritual protection)

Herbs for Tea

1 teaspoon lavender

1 teaspoon lemon balm

1 teaspoon peppermint

1 sprig fresh rosemary

A black teapot

A black cup and saucer

A white cloth

Begin by cleansing your space, crystals, teapot, cup, and herbs of any negative or stagnant energies. This can be achieved through smudging with bay leaves, sound cleansing, cleansing spray, or visualization techniques. Set your intentions and program your crystals and herbs focused on psychic protection. Be clear about your desire to shield yourself from negative energies, psychic attacks, or emotional vampirism.

Prepare and blend your tea. Create your crystal grid by setting your cup and saucer at the center of your cloth. Place a black tourmaline at each corner of the outer square grid, symbolizing grounding and strong protection. Place the smoky quartz in a diamond shape around the outside of the saucer, focusing on creating a shield against negativity. Hold the amethyst in your hand. Activate your grid by using a wand, mind, or your finger to connect each crystal. As you do this, envision a protective light emanating from the grid, encasing you in a shield that blocks negative energies.

Boil water and pour it over the blend. Allow it to steep for about 10 minutes. As it steeps, focus on your intentions, visualizing a protective barrier forming around your psychic and emotional space. Bring your hands together with the amethyst between them. Hover them above the steam, visualizing the energies charging the crystal for psychic protection. Then sip your tea, imagining its protective properties infusing your body and spirit, bolstering your psychic defenses.

After finishing your tea, spend time meditating near your crystal grid. Picture yourself surrounded by a luminous barrier that allows only positive energies to penetrate, keeping you safe and secure. Keep the amethyst as a protective charm, cleansing it and replenishing it as needed.

When the work is done, dismantle your grid, cleanse and store the crystals. Respectfully dispose of the tea leaves, perhaps by drying and keeping them close to your immediate surroundings, or by composting and burying them within your garden. This spell can be a powerful tool for those looking to safeguard their energy, prevent psychic attacks, and maintain emotional and psychic well-being. Repeat as desired, especially during times of vulnerability, when working in energetically demanding situations, or when you feel the need for an extra layer of psychic protection.

Purification Grid Remedy

This remedy is a powerful way to cleanse your energy, space, and spirit, promoting a sense of renewal and clarity. This ritual combines the purifying energies of crystals with the detoxifying properties of specific herbs to create a potent focus for clearing away negativity and stagnant energies.

GRID

Hexagram

INGREDIENTS AND TOOLS

Crystals

1 selenite plate (for cleansing and purifying energies)

3 clear quartz (to amplify energy and intentions)

3 black tourmaline (for grounding and protection against negative energy)

Herbs for Tea

1 teaspoon lemon balm
1 teaspoon roasted dandelion root
1 sprig fresh rosemary
1 teaspoon vervain
Honey

A strainer
A glass cup
Small white cloth
A slate base or designated area
Sea salt

PREPARATION

Cleanse your space and items with frankincense and myrrh, sound cleansing, cleansing spray, or visualization. Set your intention and program your crystals and herbs, focusing on purification. Be clear about what you wish to cleanse, whether it's your energy, your home, environment, or specific aspects of your life.

Prepare and blend your tea within the tea strainer in your cup. Create your crystal grid by first placing the clear quartz crystals upon the first triangle pointing up. Then set the black tourmaline crystals upon the overlapping triangle pointing down. At the center of the slate base or designated space, place the selenite base as the core of your grid, symbolizing purity and light. Restate your intentions towards cleansing, protection, and spiritual purification. Set the white cloth upon the selenite plate and place your teacup on it. Take the sea salt and outline the hexagram between the crystals.

Activate your grid by using a wand, mind, or your finger, connecting each crystal. As you do this, envision a bright light emanating from the grid, purifying everything it touches. Focus this energy to bless the tea blend. Boil water and pour it over the tea. Allow it to steep for about 10 minutes. As it steeps, focus on your intentions, visualizing all negativity and stagnant energies being washed away.

Sip your tea and visualize the tea manifesting your intentions for purification. After finishing your tea, spend time meditating near your crystal grid. See yourself and your environment surrounded by a radiant light that leaves only positivity and clarity in its wake. When your work is done, carefully dismantle your grid, cleanse and store the crystals. Gently gather the sea salt and use this to create a barrier over your thresholds.

This grid is wonderful to promote a fresh start or to heal the environment of an area. If meant to heal environmental trauma, the tea brew may be made and poured over the area.

Truth Grid Remedy

This remedy can be wonderful and insightful for those seeking clarity, honesty, and the revelation of truths in their lives. This spell combines the energy of specific crystals known for their connection to truth and communication, with a tea blend designed to enhance clarity and understanding. If seeking truth from someone else, this tea must be shared together. The following recipe is for two people.

GRID

Circle

Crystals

4 lapis lazuli (for truth and enlightenment)

3 sodalite (for communication and truth)

1 aquamarine (for courage to express truth)

Herbs for Tea

1 teaspoon dandelion root

2 teaspoons red clover

2 teaspoons chamomile

1 teaspoon licorice root

A cast-iron teapot

2 cups

A tea tray

PREPARATION

Cleanse your space and item by burning a blend of dragon's blood resin, white copal, frankincense, myrrh, and sandalwood over a charcoal disk; then open the windows and air out your space. Set your intentions and program your crystals and herbs to focus on the specific truths you wish to uncover, express, or understand more deeply.

Prepare your tea mindfully within the cast-iron teapot. Create your crystal grid by first placing the aquamarine at the top of the circle. Then, going clockwise, place a lapis lazuli crystal to the right, followed by sodalite, then lapis, then sodalite at the bottom of the circle, then lapis, sodalite, and lastly lapis. Place either one or two cups (if having company) in the center of the circle.

Activate your grid using a wand, your mind, or your finger to connect each crystal, starting from the aquamarine and moving clockwise around the circle. As you do this, envision a vibrant blue light connecting the crystals, creating a powerful union of energy centered on truth and communication. Wait for your company to arrive before brewing. Mindfully boil water and pour it over the tea, allowing it to steep for about 10 minutes. As it steeps, focus on your intentions, visualizing clarity and truth enveloping your situation. Serve the tea in the cups within the grid, focusing the energy to infuse the brew.

Sip your tea slowly, taking your time, preparing yourself for the revelation and expression of truths. Take your time in asking questions casually, working them into the conversation nonchalantly. After finishing your tea, toast to yourself, or to your guest, and visualize being surrounded by a clear, blue light. Ensure that the energy continues to inspire truth and clarity.

Carefully dismantle your grid, cleanse and store the crystals. Repeat as desired, especially during times of confusion, misunderstanding, or when making important decisions that require clear insight.

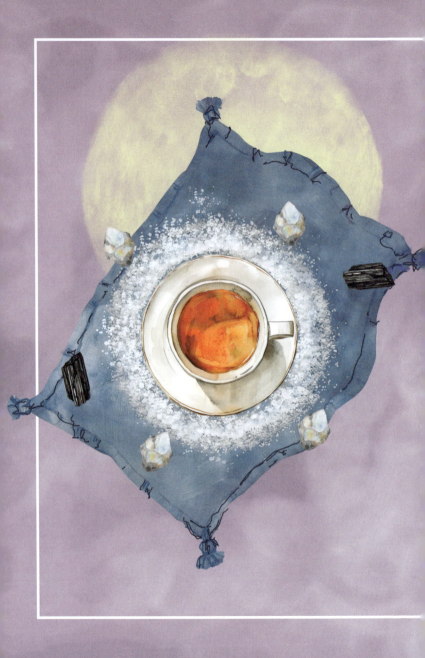

Advanced Grids: Lunar, Esbat, and Elemental Ceremonies

Advanced crystal grids go beyond simple designs. They can comprise multiples of a geometric shape (such as what is known as an Infinite Hexagram—hexagrams within hexagrams) or a shape within a shape such as a diamond within a square. These geometric shapes resonate with higher frequencies and complex intentions. They can incorporate multiple layers, types of crystals, herbs, and plants, and may be drawn with salt. These grids harness the vibrational energies of the crystals, the geometric patterns that guide the flow of energy, and the elemental power of the ceremony's focus—tea, in this case—to create a harmonious and potent field of energy.

The intricate layouts of advanced crystal grids help participants connect more deeply with the earth's energy, facilitating a greater sense of harmony, intention, and balance. These advanced geometric patterns and specific crystal layers and vibrations focus and amplify the intentions set during a ritual ceremony, making them more potent and likely to manifest faster.

These ceremonies can serve as powerful tools for healing and transformation, connecting the physical, emotional, and spiritual needs through the synergistic power of the seasons and lunar cycles. The integration of advanced crystal grids with tea ceremonies and rituals offers a profound method for enhancing the spiritual and therapeutic benefits of connecting with the natural flow of the elements. This creates a harmonious bridge between the seasons, phases of the moon, and intentions involved, leading to a more profound healing and transformative experience in the practice of tea witchery.

As always, trust in your intuition and inner guidance. While these rituals are carefully designed, they remain mere guides. If a certain crystal, pattern, tea blend, or ingredient is calling to be changed or substituted, do not hold your gifts back. Follow your inner voice and move with the flow of your own magick.

Lunar Esbat Grids

Lunar crystal tea grids combine the energy of crystals with the ritual of tea drinking, aligned with the phases of the moon, to support personal intentions and well-being. These grids are carefully arranged patterns of crystals surrounding or placed near a teacup or pot, intended to enhance the tea's energetic properties in harmony with lunar energies. The selection of crystals and tea blends below can be customized monthly based on one's specific intentions, such as promoting healing, release, enhancing intuition, beginning anew, or fostering love and prosperity. As the moon cycles through its phases, practitioners may adjust their grids to align with new goals, harnessing the moon's shifting energies for manifestation, release, or transformation. This practice offers a personalized and dynamic way to integrate the healing powers of crystals and the soothing nature of tea into a mindful ritual, attuned to both the cosmos and individual needs.

New Moon Ceremony

This New Moon ceremony is a beautiful practice to set intentions, release what no longer serves you, ward off evil, create defense spells, and connect with the energies of renewal and new beginnings. It may be used as a general guideline and the grid may be used continuously with every new moon.

INGREDIENTS AND TOOLS

Crystals
2 black tourmaline (for protection)
4 labradorite (for transformation)

Candles
2 black candles

Oils
Frankincense
Lavender
Peppermint
Coconut oil

Sea salt

New Moon Tea Recipe
1 teaspoon black tea
1 teaspoon blue mallow
1 slice lemon
1 teaspoon coconut milk
Honey or agave nectar to sweeten (optional)

Setting the Space

Cleanse the area using your preferred method for clearing negative energy. Open windows to let fresh air flow through or, if possible, perform this ceremony outdoors. Blend your oils in the coconut carrier oil and anoint the candles. You may also anoint your pulse points. In a teapot, intentionally combine the tea blend. Mindfully boil new-moon water and set near your space. Program the crystals with your intention to connect with the energies of the new moon.

Grid Layout

Create a circle with sea salt. Within the circle, place the four labradorite crystals in each direction, going from the top to the right, bottom, and left. Outside of the circle, place the black tourmaline on either side, from left to right. Place the two candles beside each black tourmaline crystal. Set your teapot within the center of the grid.

Light the candles. Activate your grid using a wand, your mind, or your finger to connect each crystal, starting from the first-laid labradorite and moving clockwise around the circle. As you do this, envision a vibrant white light connecting the crystals. Focus this white light entering and empowering the tea.

Close your eyes and take a few deep breaths to center yourself. With intent, pour the hot water over your tea and allow to steep for 4 to 5 minutes. Strain and serve yourself a cup. Hold the cup of tea close to you. Visualize your intentions for the coming lunar cycle. Imagine your goals and desires manifesting. Feel the energy of the crystals, take in the scent of the oils, and let the warmth of the tea amplify your intentions. When you feel ready, slowly drink your tea, envisioning it as a potion of manifestation, filling you with the energy and clarity to achieve your desires. Spend some time meditating on your intentions. Write them down if you feel called to or perform additional spells within this grid. Allow the candles to burn down safely. Close the ritual by expressing gratitude to the universe and yourself for this sacred time. Leave the crystal grid up until the first crescent of the new moon is visible. Be sure to deactivate the grid once the work is done. Cleanse and store safely away.

Waxing Moon Ceremony

This enriching ceremony, done during the waxing moon phase, is a lovely way to connect with the moon's growing energies, inviting abundance, growth, love, and new beginnings into your life. This ritual combines the power of crystals, candles, essential oils, and a specially crafted tea to create a sacred space for meditation and intention-setting.

INGREDIENTS AND TOOLS

Crystals
4 citrine (for abundance and positivity)
2 clear quartz (for amplification of your intentions and energies)

Candles
2 white candles
Optional substitutes: green candles for growth;
gold candles for abundance

Oils

Jasmine

Lavender

Frankincense

Sweet almond oil

Sea salt

Waxing Moon Tea Recipe

1 teaspoon white tea

1 teaspoon lemon balm

1 teaspoon dried papaya bits

1 teaspoon coconut sugar

RITUAL EXECUTION

Setting the Space

Choose a night during the waxing moon phase when the moon is visible in the sky. This phase is perfect for manifesting growth and attracting new opportunities. Find a quiet, comfortable space where you won't be disturbed. This could be indoors near a window where the moon is visible or outdoors in a garden or on a balcony. Use your preferred method to cleanse the area of any negative energy. Blend your oils using the sweet almond carrier oil and anoint the candles, setting your intentions as you do so. Focus on purification, growth, and spiritual connection. You may also anoint your pulse points. In a teapot, intentionally combine the tea blend. Mindfully boil moon water and set near your space. Program the crystals with your intention to connect with the energies of the waxing moon.

Grid Layout

Create a half circle with sea salt, with the curve side down. Place the first citrine at the center of the half circle of salt, the second crystal on the right corner, the third in the bottom of the half curve, and the fourth crystal on the left corner. Outside of the half circle, place the two clear quartz crystals on either side, from left to right. Place the two candles beside each of the clear quartz crystals. Set your teapot within the center of the grid.

Light the candles. Activate your grid using a wand, your mind, or your finger to connect each crystal, starting from the first-laid citrine and moving clockwise around the circle. As you do this, envision a vibrant yellow light connecting the crystals. Envision this light entering and empowering the tea. Pour the hot water over your tea blend. Let it steep for 3 to 5 minutes while you visualize the moon and crystal energy infusing your tea with light and power. Focus on your intentions for this ritual, whether it's personal growth, attracting abundance, or starting new projects. Serve yourself and others tea. Sit comfortably in front of your crystal grid, holding your cup of tea. Take a moment to breathe deeply, inhaling the aromas of your tea and the essential oils. Sip your tea slowly, imagining its lunar-infused energy spreading throughout your body. Visualize your intentions growing with the moon, becoming stronger and clearer with each sip.

When ready, meditate on your desires and how you plan to achieve them. Use the energy of the crystals, the light of the candles, and the essence of the tea to send your intentions out into the universe. You may do additional spell work at this point.

Once you have finished your tea and feel your intentions have been fully charged with the waxing moon's energy, express gratitude

to the moon, the earth, and the elements for their guidance and support. Snuff out the candles, in the reverse order that you lit them. Carefully dismantle your crystal grid, and cleanse and store your crystals in a safe place until your next ritual. Remember, the power of this ritual comes from your intentions and the energies you tap into. Feel free to modify any part of this ritual to better suit your personal practice and preferences.

Full Moon Ceremony

This magickal ritual is designed to enhance your spiritual connection and promote healing, love, and success as you harness the potent energies of the full moon. It's a powerful way to connect with the cosmic energies, set intentions, and promote inner growth and healing. Every month the full moon presents opportunities for you to set different intentions. Feel free to customize the crystal types, tea ingredients, and essential oils to match your personal preferences and needs. Crystals may be swapped out, candle colors changed, or herbs added to the tea recipe.

INGREDIENTS AND TOOLS

Flower of Life template

Crystals

6 moonstone (for intuition)

4 selenite (for clarity)

6 amethyst (for spiritual growth)

20 clear quartz (amplify energy)

Candles
2 silver candles

Oils
Frankincense
Lavender
Olive oil

Sea salt

Full Moon Tea Recipe
1 teaspoon green tea
1 teaspoon jasmine
1 teaspoon chickweed
1 teaspoon coconut milk

RITUAL EXECUTION

Setting the Space
Begin by cleansing your space and yourself to clear any negative energies. You can use incense, sound vibrations from a singing bowl, cleansing spray, or visual techniques. Blend your oils in the olive carrier oil and anoint the candles, setting your intentions as you do so. Focus on your desires: abundance, love, or health. You may also

anoint your pulse points. In a teapot, intentionally combine the tea blend. Mindfully boil full-moon water and set near your space. With your intention, program the crystals to connect with the energies of the full moon.

Grid Layout

On a colored cloth that represents your intentions, arrange the sea salt in a circular pattern, creating a boundary. Lay the template on the cloth. Place your cup or teapot in the center of the grid. With focused intent, lay six moonstones on the inner petals around the cup. Lay the six amethyst crystals in the center of the next row of flowers. Then lay the remaining clear quartz on the outer petals. Lastly, place a selenite at each cardinal point. Lay out these crystals to what pleases your intuition, letting it guide you. Place the two silver candles on the outside of the grid, from left to right.

Light the candles. Activate your grid by using a wand, mind, or your finger to connect each crystal, starting from the first-laid moonstone and moving clockwise around the circle. As you do this, visualize the full moon's light charging the grid. Envision a vibrant silver light connecting the crystals. Envision this light entering and empowering the tea. Pour the hot water over your tea blend. Let it steep for 1 to 3 minutes, visualizing the moon and crystal energy infusing your tea with light and power. Focus on your intentions for this ritual. Serve yourself and others tea. Sit comfortably, gazing at your candlelit grid through softly focused eyes, holding your cup of tea.

Close your eyes, take deep breaths, and center yourself. Sip your tea slowly, imagining the energy of the full moon flowing through you, connecting you to the universe. Meditate on your intentions, visualizing them coming to fruition with the help of the moon's energy. When ready, use this time to achieve any other spell work while the grid is activated. Close the ritual by giving thanks to the moon, the universe, and your crystals for their guidance and energy. Snuff out the candles and leave your crystal grid up overnight to continue absorbing the full moon's energy. You may place any tools or blends within the grid to charge as well. Wait till the next evening to deactivate your grid. Cleanse and store them safely away.

Waning Moon Ceremony

This ceremony harnesses the energies of the waning moon. It involves intention, natural elements, and a serene environment. This ritual aims to promote release, banishment, gratitude, divination, and introspection. This ritual can be a deeply personal and transformative experience, helping to align your energy with the moon's cycles and the natural world. Divination work is highly recommended.

INGREDIENTS AND TOOLS

Crystals
4 moonstone (for intuition)
2 black tourmaline (for grounding and protection)

Candles
2 gray candles

Oils
Lavender

Clary sage

Frankincense

Castor oil

Sea salt

Waning Moon Tea Recipe

1 teaspoon oolong tea

1 teaspoon willow bark

1 teaspoon marshmallow root

1 teaspoon coconut sugar

RITUAL EXECUTION

Setting the Space

Begin by meditating on your intention for this ritual. The waning moon is a time for letting go, reflection, and preparation for new beginnings. Cleanse your space and yourself to clear any negative energies. You can use incense, sound vibrations from a singing bowl, cleansing spray, or visual techniques. Blend your oils in the castor carrier oil and anoint the candles, setting your intentions as you do so. You may also anoint your pulse points. In a teapot, intentionally combine the tea blend. Mindfully boil moon water and set near your space. With your intention, program the crystals to connect with the energies of the waning moon.

Grid Layout

Create a half circle with sea salt, with the curved side up. Place the first moonstone at the center of the half circle of salt, the second crystal on the left corner, the third on the top of the half curve, and

the fourth crystal on the right corner. Outside of the half circle, place the black tourmaline on either side, from top to bottom. Place the two candles beside each of the black tourmaline crystals. Set your teapot within the center of the grid.

Light the candles with mindfulness, dedicating each flame to your intention. Activate your grid using a wand, your mind, or your finger to connect each crystal, starting from the first-laid moonstone and moving clockwise around the circle. As you do this, envision a vibrant light connecting the crystals. Envision this light entering and empowering the tea. Pour the hot water over your tea blend. Let it steep for 3 to 5 minutes, visualizing the waning moon's energy infusing into the brew. Focus on your intentions for this ritual. Hold your hands over the cup, infusing your own energy and intentions into the tea.

Serve yourself and others tea. Sip your tea slowly, envisioning it washing away what no longer serves you, cleansing your body and spirit. While drinking your tea, reflect on what you wish to release. Visualize these things dissipating with the waning moon's light. Express gratitude to the moon, the crystals, and the elements for their guidance and energy. Use this time to perform any additional spell work.

Once you have finished your tea, take a moment to sit in silence, acknowledging the shift within. Extinguish the candles safely, thanking each for its light. Collect your crystals, gently cleanse them, and store them until your next ritual. In the days that follow, carry a piece of moonstone with you to remind you of your intentions and to keep connecting with the waning moon's energy. Reflect on the changes you experience and write them down in a journal.

Blue Moon Ceremony

This blue moon ceremony can be a profound and powerful experience. This ritual is designed to help you connect with the heightened energies of the blue moon, using the power of crystals, candles, essential oils, and a specially crafted tea blend to enhance your spiritual connection and inner reflection. It may also instill wisdom, wealth, health, love, protection, strength, and psychic development. Remember, intention is key in any ritual, so approach this practice with a clear, focused mind and an open heart. You may customize this grid to your desired intent.

INGREDIENTS AND TOOLS

Seed of Life template

Crystals

6 moonstone (for intuition and connection to the moon)

6 labradorite (for transformation and magickal energy)

4 selenite (for clarity and cleansing)

6 clear quartz (for amplification of your intentions)

Candles

2 blue candles

Oils

Lavender

Chamomile

Frankincense

Grapeseed oil

Sea salt

Blue Moon Tea Recipe

¼ teaspoon mugwort

¼ teaspoon goldenrod

1 teaspoon blue mallow

1 teaspoon mullein

Honey

RITUAL EXECUTION

Setting the Space

Choose a quiet, comfortable space where you won't be disturbed. Ideally, this should be a place where you can see the moon or feel its presence. Cleanse your space and yourself to clear any negative energies. You can use incense, sound vibrations from a singing bowl, cleansing spray, or visual techniques. Blend your oils in the grapeseed carrier oil and anoint the candles, setting your intentions as you do so. You may also anoint your pulse points. In a teapot, intentionally combine the tea blend. Mindfully boil moon water and set near your space. Program the crystals with your intention to connect with the energies of the blue moon.

Grid Layout

On a colored cloth that represents your intentions, arrange the sea salt in a circular pattern, creating a boundary. Lay the template on the cloth. Place your cup or teapot in the center of the grid. With focused intent, lay six moonstones on the inner petals around the cup. Lay the six labradorite crystals in the center of the next row of flowers. Then lay the remaining clear quartz on the outer petals. Lastly, place a selenite at each cardinal point. Lay out these crystals to what pleases

your intuition, letting it guide you. Place the two blue candles on the outside of the grid, from left to right.

Light the candles. Activate your grid using a wand, your mind, or your finger to connect each crystal, starting from the first-laid moonstone and moving clockwise around the circle. As you do this, visualize the blue moon's light charging the grid. Envision a vibrant blue-white light connecting the crystals. Envision this light entering and empowering the tea. Pour the hot water over your tea blend. Let it steep for 5 to 10 minutes while you visualize the moon and crystal energy infusing your tea with light and power. Focus on your intentions for this ritual. Serve yourself and others tea. Sit comfortably, gazing at your candlelit grid through softly focused eyes, holding your cup of tea. Meditate on your intention, visualize it coming to fruition, and feel the energies of the crystals, the moon, and the tea guiding and supporting your spiritual journey. Use this time to do any additional spell work, using the grid to amplify the energy.

Once you have finished your tea, take a moment to thank the moon, the crystals, and the elements for their guidance and energy. The grid may remain activated until the following evening. Be sure to cleanse and store away your crystals properly. Respectfully dispose of your tea remains depending on your intent. Be sure to drink plenty of water to help integrate the energies and to aid in the release of any toxins. Journal about your experience, noting any insights, visions, or feelings that arose during the ritual.

Eclipse Ceremony

This powerful tea ritual will help you to connect with the energies of a solar eclipse. It is specially crafted to enhance spiritual connection and introspection, fostering a deep bond with the celestial energies and your inner self. Remember to approach it with an open heart and a clear intention for the best experience. This is for all matters of transformative intentions, strength, courage, abundance, harmony, healing, wish magick, conjuring, deep inner work, and emotional cleansing.

INGREDIENTS AND TOOLS

Seed of Life template

Crystals

6 moonstone (for lunar connection)

8 sunstone (for transformation)

6 clear quartz (for amplification of energy)

6 amethyst (for intuition)

Candles

2 white candles

Oils

Frankincense

Clary sage

Jasmine

Sunflower oil

Eclipse Tea Recipe

1 teaspoon pu-erh tea

1 teaspoon dried lemon peel

1 teaspoon dried orange peel

1 vanilla bean

Honey

RITUAL EXECUTION

Setting the Space

Choose a quiet, comfortable space where you won't be disturbed. Ideally, this should be a place where you can be under the eclipse as it is happening or feel its presence. Cleanse your space and yourself to clear any negative energies. You can use incense, sound vibrations from a singing bowl, cleansing spray, or visual techniques. Blend your oils in the sunflower carrier oil and anoint the candles, setting your intentions as you do so. Anoint yourself on your wrists, forehead, and heart. This opens your energy fields and sets the intention for connecting deeply with the lunar eclipse energies. In a teapot, intentionally combine the tea blend. Mindfully boil a mix of half moon water and half solar water, then set near your space. With your intention, program the crystals to connect with the energies of the eclipse.

Grid Layout

This grid will be a blend of the Seed of Life and a sunburst. On a colored cloth that represents your intentions, lay the template on the cloth. Place your cup or teapot in the center of the grid. With focused intent, lay the six moonstones on the inner petals around the cup. Lay the six amethyst crystals in the center of the next row of flowers. Then lay the remaining clear quartz on the outer petals. Lastly, create a sunburst pattern with the sunstones, pointing outward. Lay out these crystals to what pleases your intuition, letting it guide you. Place the two white candles on the outside of the grid, from left to right.

Light the candles to invite warmth and light, symbolizing the eclipse's energy. Activate your grid using a wand, your mind, or your finger to connect each crystal, starting from the first-laid moonstone and moving clockwise around the circle, then bursting out. As you do this, visualize your intentions for this ritual—be it clarity, transformation, or release—charging the grid. Envision a vibrant white-golden light connecting the crystals. Envision this light entering and empowering the tea. Pour the hot water over your tea blend. Let it steep for 3 to 5 minutes, visualizing the eclipse and crystal energy infusing your tea with light and power. Focus on your intentions for this ritual. Serve yourself and others tea. Sit comfortably, gazing at your candlelit grid through softly focused eyes, holding your cup of tea. Meditate on your intention, visualize it coming to fruition, and feel the energies of the crystals, the eclipse, and the tea empowering and manifesting your desires. Use this time to do any additional spell work, using the grid to amplify the energy.

Close your eyes, take deep breaths, and center yourself. Sip your tea slowly, letting its warmth and energy spread throughout your body. With each sip, imagine the eclipse's transformative energy flowing within you, guiding you toward deeper understanding and clarity, opening the doorways to new opportunities. Meditate on your intentions, letting the energy of the crystals, the scent of the oils, the light of the candles, and the essence of the tea guide your thoughts and emotions. Visualize the eclipse enveloping you in its powerful energy, catalyzing growth and healing.

Once you feel your ritual is complete, express gratitude to the moon, the crystals, and the elements for their guidance and energy. Snuff out the candles, grounding yourself back into the present moment. Keep the grid activated until the eclipse has ended. Then cleanse and store the crystals safely.

Sabbat Grids

New Year's Ceremony

This grid welcomes the New Year, incorporating elements to manifest renewal, protection, prosperity, and intuition that can create a powerful new beginning. Best when done at the stroke of midnight, or in the morning of the new year.

GRID

Twelve-Pointed Star (double merkaba)

INGREDIENTS AND TOOLS

Crystals

3 sunstone

3 moonstone

3 black tourmaline

3 selenite

3 fire agate (Fire)

3 smoky quartz (Earth)
3 clear quartz (Air)
3 aquamarine (Water)
6 amethyst

Candles

3 white candles

New Year's Tea Recipe

1 teaspoon green tea
1 teaspoon holy basil
1 teaspoon chamomile
1 teaspoon spearmint

Teapot
Cups
White cloth

RITUAL EXECUTION

Setting the Space

Choose a quiet, comfortable area where you won't be disturbed. Cleanse this space with your preferred method: you can use incense, sound vibrations from a singing bowl, cleansing spray, or visual techniques. In a teapot, intentionally combine the tea blend. Mindfully boil water, then set near your space. Program the crystals with your intention to connect with the energies of the new year.

Grid Layout

Lay out the template upon the white cloth. Place your teapot with the herbal blend in the center. Starting at the left-hand side (10 o'clock position on the template), lay the sunstone on each point of the first large triangle. Move downward, counterclockwise, to the next triangle, and lay the moonstone. Move to the next triangle and place the black tourmaline. Lay the selenite crystals on the remaining outer points to draw in assistance from the higher realms.

Lay an air crystal on the V inside the first triangle point between the sunstone and moonstone. Move to the next triangle point and lay a water crystal on the V inside the second triangle between the moonstone and black tourmaline. Move to the next triangle point and lay a fire crystal on the V inside the third triangle between the black tourmaline and selenite. Move to the next triangle point and lay an earth crystal on the V inside the triangle point between the selenite and Sunstone. Continue this pattern with the crystals around the grid: Air, Water, Fire, and Earth. Lay the six amethyst crystals within to form an inner hexagon around the teapot.

As you place each crystal, set an intention for what it represents.

"May this sunstone bring new light and opportunities.
May this moonstone enhance my gifts and intuition.
May this black tourmaline protect my endeavors and path.
May this selenite connect me to my higher goals and self.
May this amethyst protect my spirit in the coming year.
May I be connected and guided by the elements."

Light the candles to invite new beginnings and growth, symbolizing the new year's energy. Activate your grid by using a wand, mind, or your finger to connect each crystal, starting from the first-laid crystal and moving clockwise around the grid. As you do this, visualize your intentions for this ritual. You may vocalize your intentions. Envision a vibrant white light connecting the crystals. Envision this light entering and empowering the tea. Pour the hot water over your tea blend. Let it steep for 3 to 5 minutes, visualizing the crystal energy infusing your tea with light and power. Serve yourself and others tea. Sit comfortably and take a moment to meditate on the past year. Acknowledge your growth and the challenges you've overcome, holding your cup of tea close to your heart. Meditate on your new intentions for the year, visualize them coming to fruition, and feel the energies of the crystals and the tea empowering and manifesting your desires.

Close your eyes, take deep breaths, and center yourself. Sip your tea slowly, letting its warmth and energy spread throughout your body, imagining its properties and the energy of the crystals infusing your body and spirit with their qualities. You can use tarot cards to gain insights into the coming year or simply spend this time in quiet reflection. Ask them what is manifesting and the obstacles you might face, and ask for answers to overcome them. Afterwards, use this time to do any additional spell work, using the grid to amplify the energy.

Once you feel your ritual is complete, express gratitude to the crystals, the elements for their guidance and energy, your chosen deities or ancestors, and the universe. Snuff out the candles, grounding yourself back into the present moment. Keep the grid activated for the remainder of the day. Then carefully dismantle the grid, cleanse the crystals, and store them safely. You may keep one of the crystals and the dried tea in a sachet and store them in a place where they can continue to bring you their benefits throughout the year. Then by the end of the new year, you may dispose of the tea leaves back to the earth, as a symbolic gesture of returning what you've taken and completing the cycle. Cleanse and store the crystal for future use.

This ceremony is a powerful way to set your intentions for the New Year, combining the energies of crystals and the ritual of tea drinking. However, always remember, the most important aspect is your intention and focus, so feel free to adapt this ceremony to best suit your spiritual path and personal preferences.

Imbolc Ceremony

Imbolc is a time of renewal, purification, and the first hints of spring. It's a perfect occasion for a tea crystal ceremony focused on awakening, growth, and the nurturing of new endeavors. This ceremony will weave together the energies of specific crystals and herbal teas to honor this sabbat.

GRID

The Dragon's Eye (tetrahedron)

INGREDIENTS AND TOOLS

Crystals (appropriate amount of each)
Garnet
Snowflake obsidian
1 clear quartz plate

Candles

2 white candles

1 green candle

Imbolc Tea Recipe

1 teaspoon white tea

1 teaspoon mint

2 teaspoons dried blackberries

1 teaspoon nettle

1 teaspoon jasmine

1 teaspoon lavender

Teapot

Cups

Light purple cloth

Incense

Lavender

Rosemary

RITUAL EXECUTION

Setting the Space

Choose a quiet, comfortable area where you won't be disturbed. Cleanse this space with the method you prefer. You can use the incense provided, sound vibrations from a singing bowl, cleansing spray, or visual techniques. Mindfully blend your tea, and heat your water as you reflect on what you wish to purify, release, or initiate in your life during Imbolc, then set near your space. With your intention, program the crystals to connect with the energies of the Imbolc.

Grid Layout

Lay out your cloth and the appropriate template of the grid. Lay the clear quartz plate at the center. Place the teapot on top of this plate, with the tea blend nearby. Place the appropriate amount of garnet crystals around the outer triangle, on the upper arms of the Y, and on the tail of the Y. Between the garnet, intersperse the appropriate amount of snowflake obsidian crystals. Place the two white candles on the top two points and place the green candle on the bottom point.

Light your candles and incense to symbolize the return of the light as days begin to grow longer. Activate your grid by using a wand, mind, or your finger to connect each crystal, starting from the first-laid crystal, and moving clockwise around the grid. As you do this, visualize your intentions for this ritual. You may vocalize your intentions. Envision a vibrant white-green-violet light connecting the crystals. Take your tea blend and gather 1 to 2 teaspoons in your palm. Bring your hands together and concentrate on clearing away the old to make room for new growth. Sprinkle your tea blend into the teapot, visualizing it like seeds being planted. Pour the water over the tea, envisioning the water being infused with your intentions as well as the energy from your crystal grid. Steep for 2 to 4 minutes.

Sit comfortably before your crystal tea grid, focusing on the light of the candle and what it represents. Allow yourself a moment of quiet meditation to feel the presence of your crystals and the warmth of the tea. Serve and begin to sip your tea, visualizing its warmth and energy spreading throughout your body, awakening and purifying as it goes. Contemplate your intentions for the coming season. What seeds (literal or metaphorical) are you planting? How do you wish to grow? Visualize these intentions being nurtured and coming to fruition. If you wish, use this time for divination or to read a passage or poem that resonates with Imbolc's themes of renewal and awakening.

As you finish your tea, give thanks to the elements, the earth, and any deities or spirits you work with for their guidance and protection. Carefully dismantle your grid, cleansing each crystal. You may wish to keep them on your altar or in a place where they can continue to support your intentions. Extinguish your candles safely, and if possible, offer the tea leaves back to the earth by using it as fertilizer or compost for your garden, closing the cycle and grounding your intentions in the physical world.

This ceremony for Imbolc combines the quiet, introspective energy of the season with the promise of renewal and growth. Tailor the ceremony to reflect your personal path and the specific energies you wish to bring into your life during this potent time of the year.

Ostara Ceremony

Ostara, the spring equinox, is a time of balance, renewal, and the burgeoning of life. It celebrates new beginnings, fertility, and growth. This ceremony for Ostara is meant to beautifully encapsulate these themes, combining the rejuvenating power of crystals and tea to set intentions for the season.

GRID

Infinite Hexagram

INGREDIENTS AND TOOLS

Crystals

3 carnelian

3 rose quartz

6 green aventurine

3 citrine

3 clear quartz

Candles

2 yellow candles

2 green candles

Incense

Lilac

Honeysuckle

Jasmine

Ostara Tea Recipe

1 teaspoon white tea

½ teaspoon hibiscus

1 teaspoon jasmine

½ teaspoon rose hips

1 teaspoon lemon balm

2 teaspoons dried raspberries

A green or pastel cloth

A spring-themed teapot

Cups

Spring flowers

RITUAL EXECUTION

Setting the Space

Cleanse a special space with the method you prefer. You can use the incense provided, sound vibrations from a singing bowl, cleansing spray, or visual techniques. Mindfully blend your tea in the teapot and heat your water as you meditate on the themes of Ostara—rebirth, renewal, and balance. Reflect on what areas of your life you'd like to grow and flourish, then set the tea near your space. With your intention, program the crystals to connect with the energies of the Ostara.

Grid Layout

Lay your cloth in your chosen space. In the center, place your spring-themed teapot to symbolize Ostara and the essence of new beginnings. Arrange the three carnelian and three rose quartz on the inner hexagram. Lay the six green aventurine on the next hexagram. Lay

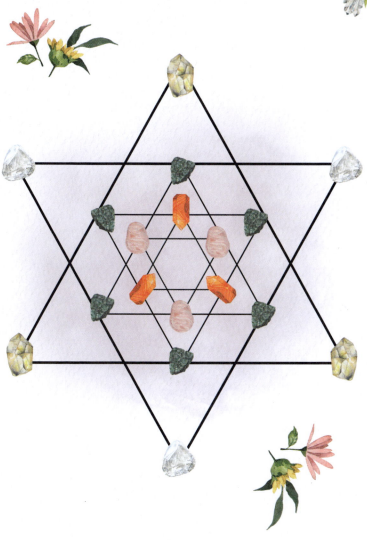

the three citrine and clear quartz crystals on the outer hexagram. You may decorate the boundary of the grid with beautiful seasonal spring flowers. Arrange the candles around the grid. This arrangement channels the season's balanced energies into your intentions. As you set each crystal, focus on your specific wishes and intentions for each area (love, growth, abundance, etc.).

Light your candles and incense to symbolize the sun's growing strength and the balance of light and dark. This act also honors the Fire element, bringing warmth and energy to your intentions. Activate your grid by using a wand, mind, or your finger to connect each crystal, starting from the first-laid crystal and moving clockwise around the grid. As you do this, visualize your intentions for this ritual. You may vocalize your intentions. Envision a vibrant pastel light connecting the crystals. Focus this energy into your teapot and blend. Pour the water over the tea, letting the steam and aroma fill the space, carrying your intentions through. Let it steep for 2 to 4 minutes. As it steeps, visualize your life blooming with vigor and energy.

Sit comfortably before your crystal tea grid, gazing at the candlelight. Allow yourself a moment of silence to feel connected with the rebirth and growth energies of Ostara. Slowly sip your tea, visualizing its essence nurturing your body and spirit, much like the earth nurtures seeds into sprouting. With each sip, imagine your intentions beginning to sprout and grow. Contemplate the balance in your life and in nature. Think about how you can bring more balance into your personal growth, relationships, and endeavors. You may wish to write down your intentions on pieces of paper and place them under the crystals for added focus and energy. You may use this time to do any additional spell work within the grid.

Once you've finished your tea and practice, express gratitude to the earth, the elements, and any deities or guides you work with for their support and guidance. Carefully dismantle your grid, cleansing each crystal. You might want to keep them near you in the coming days or place them in parts of your home where their energies can aid in manifesting your intentions. Snuff out the candle, mindful of the balance between light and dark, and how both are necessary for growth. If possible, offer the tea leaves back to the earth as a gesture of gratitude and completion of the cycle. Or you may make a weaker brew and use it to water your garden to continue the magick.

Beltane Ceremony

Beltane, celebrated on May 1st, is a fire festival that marks the peak of spring and the beginning of summer. This sabbat honors fertility, growth, passion, and the union of the Goddess and the God. This ceremony for Beltane can beautifully incorporate these themes, blending the invigorating power of crystals with the gentle, nurturing essence of tea to set intentions for vibrant growth and joyful abundance.

GRID

Merkaba (star tetrahedron)

INGREDIENTS AND TOOLS

Crystals
3 red jasper
5 malachite

3 emerald

5 rose quartz

Crystal wand

Candles

2 red

1 green

Beltane Tea Recipe

1 teaspoon rooibos

1 teaspoon calendula

1 teaspoon hibiscus

2 teaspoons dried strawberries

Pinch of mint

Red cloth

Teapot

Cups

RITUAL EXECUTION

Setting the Space

Choose an outdoor space, if possible, to connect directly with the energy of the earth and the burgeoning life around you. If indoors, choose a space with natural light and fresh air. Cleanse this space energetically with incense, sound, or cleansing spray, inviting in positive, vibrant energy. Mindfully blend your tea in the teapot and heat your water as you meditate on Beltane's themes—fertility, passion, and joy. Consider what you wish to "grow" in your life. Set this near your space. With your intention, program the crystals to connect with the energies of the Beltane.

Grid Layout

Lay your red cloth on the ground or table and set down the template. In the center, place the teapot to act as the heart of your grid, symbolizing the love and unity celebrated at Beltane. Outline the largest upward-pointing triangle with three rose quartz for heart-balancing energy. Outline the largest downward-pointing triangle with three red jasper for grounding. Lay three malachite on the inner downward-pointing triangle for love and transformation. Lay emerald crystals at each point of the inner triangle, for fertility. Intuitively place the remaining crystals on any empty connecting lines. Place the two red candles on either side of the grid, and the green candle at the top point. This arrangement channels the dynamic and fertile energies of Beltane into your intentions. As you place each crystal, focus on your desires for growth, passion, and joy in the coming season.

Light your candles to honor the fire of Beltane, symbolizing the sun's growing power and the fire of passion and creativity. Activate your grid by using the crystal wand to connect each crystal, starting from the first-laid crystal, and moving clockwise around the grid. As you do this, visualize your intentions for this ritual. You may vocalize your intentions. Envision a bright red light connecting the crystals. Focus this energy into your teapot and blend. Pour the water over the tea, letting the aroma and warmth envelop you, carrying your intentions throughout your sacred space. Let it steep for 5 to 10 minutes. As you steep the tea, visualize your intentions taking root.

Sit comfortably before your crystal tea grid, focusing on the flames and across the crystals with soft eyes, allowing yourself to feel enveloped in warmth and love. Sip your tea, imagining its essence infusing your body with the energy of growth and the fulfillment of your desires. With each sip, visualize your intentions blossoming. Contemplate the fertile energy of the earth. Think about how you can nurture and tend to your dreams and projects, just as a gardener tends to their garden. You may use this time to do additional spell work.

Once you've finished your tea and feel your intentions have been fully embraced, express gratitude to the earth, the elements, and any deities or guides you work with for their support and energy. Carefully dismantle your grid, cleansing each crystal. These crystals can be kept close in the days to come or placed in your environment where they can best support your intentions. Extinguish the candles, reflecting on the balance of light and warmth that nurtures all life. If possible, return the tea leaves to the earth as a gesture of gratitude and completion, or you may dry them and save to burn in the sacred bonfires of Beltane.

Litha Ceremony

Litha, also known as midsummer or the summer solstice, is the peak of the summer and the longest day of the year. This sabbat celebrates the sun at its strongest, emphasizing abundance, growth, and the power of the light. This ceremony for Litha can capture these themes, combining the energizing power of crystals with the refreshing qualities of herbal tea to amplify intentions of prosperity, vitality, and success. This ceremony is best done when the sun is at its peak.

GRID

Multiarmed Spiral

INGREDIENTS AND TOOLS

Crystals
8 citrine
8 sunstone

Candles
Yellow or gold candles

Incense
Mugwort
Chamomile
Lavender

Litha Tea Recipe
1 teaspoon green tea
1 teaspoon peppermint
1 teaspoon elder flowers

1 teaspoon chamomile

1 teaspoon echinacea

2 teaspoons dried cantaloupe melon bits

Yellow or gold cloth

Teapot

Cups

Yellow or orange flowers

RITUAL EXECUTION

Setting the Space

Ideally, this ceremony should be held outdoors on the ground, to directly soak in the sun's energy, but if that's not possible, choose a bright, sunny room on a tea tray, wood, slate, or marble piece. Cleanse this space energetically with incense, sweetgrass, or sound, inviting in the vibrant, life-giving energy of the sun. Mindfully blend your tea in the teapot and boil your water as you contemplate the power of the sun and its life-giving energy. Reflect on what areas of your life you'd like to energize and grow. Set this kettle near your space. With your intention, program the crystals to connect with the energies of the summer solstice.

Grid Layout

Lay your yellow or gold cloth on the ground or table. In the center, place the teapot to act as a beacon of pure energy, magnifying your intentions. Lay the citrine and sunstone on every other arm, alternately going outward, radiating energy. This arrangement embodies the full cycle and power of the sun throughout the day. As you place each crystal, focus on the abundance, vitality, and success you wish to bring into your life. Lay out the yellow and/or orange flowers on the arms that are empty. Fill in the spaces. Arrange your candles safely around the grid.

Light your candles and incense as a tribute to the sun, recognizing its peak power at Litha and its role in nurturing life. Activate your grid by using the crystal wand to connect each crystal, starting from the first-laid crystal and moving clockwise around the grid. As you do this, visualize your intentions for this ritual. You may vocalize your intentions. Envision a bright gold light connecting the crystals. Focus this energy into your teapot and blend. Acknowledge the tea's solar connections and invite calm and clarity into your ceremony. Pour the water over the tea, letting its warmth remind you of the sun's embrace, spreading throughout your sacred space. Let it steep for 2 to 4 minutes. As you steep the tea, visualize the sun's light filling the brew with vibrant energy.

Sit comfortably before your crystal tea grid, absorbing the light of the candles and the symbolic central spiral in your grid. Allow yourself a moment of silence to feel connected with the sun's energy and your surroundings. Sip your tea, imagining its essence revitalizing every cell in your body with the sun's warmth and energy. With each sip, visualize your intentions growing stronger and more vibrant. Contemplate the abundance and growth around you. Think about how you can harness this energy to nurture your own projects, dreams, and well-being. You may use this time to do additional spell work or practice.

Once you've finished your tea and feel your intentions have been fully charged by the sun's energy, express gratitude to the earth, the

sun, the elements, and any deities or guides you work with for their support and vitality. Carefully dismantle your grid, cleansing each crystal. Consider keeping them in a sunny spot in the days following the ceremony to continue drawing on the sun's vibrant energy. Extinguish the candles, contemplating the balance of light and darkness, and how both are essential for growth. If possible, offer the tea leaves back to the earth as an expression of gratitude and completion. Or you may dry and incorporate them into other bakery items.

Lammas Ceremony

Lammas, also known as Lughnasadh, celebrated on August 1st, marks the beginning of the harvest season. This sabbat is a time of gratitude, abundance, and reaping what we have sown, both literally and metaphorically. This ceremony for Lammas can encapsulate these themes, combining the nurturing essence of tea with the grounding power of crystals to set intentions for harvesting, gratitude, and preparing for the transition into autumn.

GRID

The Labyrinth

INGREDIENTS AND TOOLS

Crystals
(a sufficient number to lay along the lines of the whole labyrinth)
Moss agate
Citrine
1 golden quartz

Candles
Orange or gold

Lammas Tea Recipe
1 teaspoon chamomile

1 teaspoon rose hips

1 teaspoon nettle

2 teaspoons dried cherries

1 cinnamon stick

Green cloth

Teapot

Cups

RITUAL EXECUTION

Setting the Space

Choose a space that feels comfortable and serene, ideally with a connection to the earth if outdoors is an option. If inside, consider bringing in elements of nature like flowers, grains, or fruits to honor the harvest. Cleanse this space energetically with incense, sound, or cleansing spray, inviting in a sense of abundance and gratitude. Blend your tea in the teapot and boil your water as you meditate on the themes of Lammas—gratitude, harvest, and the cycle of growth. Reflect on the fruits of your own labors and what you are now harvesting in your life. Mindfully pour your hot water over your tea. As you steep the tea, visualize the golden warmth of the sun nurturing all that you have cultivated. Steep for 5 to 10 minutes. With your intentions, program the crystals to connect with the energies of Lammas.

Grid Layout

The labyrinth is a grid that can be of your own design, taking the shape—square or circular—and containing as many twists and turns as you desire. The labyrinth symbolizes a journey to a destination—what that "destination" is will be guided by your intuition.

Lay your green cloth on the ground or table and the grid template upon it. Light your candles to honor the sun and its vital role in bringing the harvest to fruition. Sit comfortably before your crystal grid, focusing on the flames and then on the labyrinth itself, allowing yourself to feel connected with the sun's energy, the abundance of the harvest, and the deep, inward path you will partake in. Begin at the labyrinth's entrance point. "Walk" the labyrinth with your mind, placing each moss agate and citrine crystal alternate. As you place each crystal, focus on the blessings and abundance you wish to acknowledge and bring into your life. Connect and channel the energies of abundance, gratitude, and transition into your intentions. Take your time to examine all that you have done to reach this harvest, what you need to continue to do, and what you have been awarded.

Once you get to the center—the destination—place the golden quartz as a beacon of concentrated energy, embodying the essence of the sun and the golden fields of grain. Sit back and take long, deep breaths, taking a moment to rest from the "journey." Serve yourself tea, and sip slowly, imagining its essence filling you with gratitude and the richness of the earth. With each sip, visualize your intentions ripening and coming to fullness. Contemplate the cycle of growth and the importance of acknowledging and giving thanks for the abundance in your life. Evaluate deeply the thoughts and feelings you had while traveling the labyrinth. You may wish to write down what you are grateful for or what you hope to harvest in the coming months on pieces of paper—place these under the central golden quartz for added focus and manifestation energy.

Once you've finished your tea and feel your intentions have been fully honored, express gratitude to the earth, the sun, the elements, and any deities or guides for their support and abundance. Carefully dismantle your grid, cleansing each crystal. These crystals can be kept in your immediate environment or carried with you so they can continue to support your intentions and serve as reminders of your gratitude and the abundance yet to come. Extinguish the candles, reflecting on the balance of light and darkness, and how both are essential for the cycle of growth and harvest. If possible, offer the tea leaves back to the earth as an expression of gratitude and completion.

Mabon Ceremony

Mabon, also known as the autumn equinox, is a time of balance between day and night before we enter the darker half of the year. It's a period for giving thanks, reflecting on the balance in our lives, and preparing for the introspective time of winter. This ceremony for Mabon merges the reflective quality of tea with the stabilizing energies of crystals to set intentions for gratitude, balance, and harmony. The best time to do this ceremony is at sunset.

GRID

Tree of Life (kabbalistic tree)

Crystals

2 tiger's eye

2 moss agate

2 aventurine

1 obsidian

1 clear quartz

1 smoky quartz

Candles

Red, orange, or brown

Mabon Tea Recipe

1 teaspoon oolong tea

1 teaspoon chamomile

1 teaspoon rose hips

1 teaspoon dried apple pieces

1 cinnamon stick

Orange or brown cloth

Teapot

Cups

Setting the Space

Choose a space that feels calm and balanced, ideally outdoors where you can be surrounded by the changing colors of nature. If inside, consider decorating your space with autumn leaves, acorns, or pine cones to reflect the season. Cleanse this space energetically with either incense, cinnamon, sound bowls, or cleansing sprays, inviting peace and equilibrium. Mindfully blend your tea within your teapot, acknowledging the strength and stability it brings. Boil water as you meditate on the themes of Mabon—balance, gratitude, and transition. Consider the balance within your own life and the areas you wish to harmonize. Program the crystals with your intentions to connect with the energies of the autumn equinox.

Grid Layout

Lay your orange or brown cloth on the ground or table. Place the teapot at the base of the Tree of Life, as a beacon of pure energy, embodying the essence of balance and clarity. Proceed up the tree, and place the two tiger's eye on either side of the first two circles. Lay the two moss agate on either side of the middle circles. Place the two aventurine on either side of the top two circles. Place clear quartz in the top circle. Lay the smoky quartz in the middle. Then place the obsidian on the bottom circle within the triangle above the teapot. This arrangement anchors the energies of balance, gratitude, and preparation into your intentions. As you place each crystal, focus on the harmony and abundance you wish to cultivate in your life. Arrange the candles around the grid. You may decorate the Tree however you like with autumn leaves, acorns, etc.

Light your candles to honor the equinox and the balance between light and darkness. Activate your grid by using a crystal wand, your mind, or your hands to connect each crystal, starting from the first-laid crystal and moving clockwise around the grid. As you do this, visualize your intentions for this ritual. You may vocalize your intentions. Envision a bright orange-brown light connecting the crystals. Focus this energy into your teapot and blend. Pour the water over the tea. Let it steep for 3 to 4 minutes. As you steep the tea, visualize grounding yourself firmly within the earth.

Sit comfortably before your crystal tea grid, focusing on the flames and on the everlasting energy of the Tree, allowing yourself to feel connected with the energies of balance and clarity. Sip your tea, imagining its essence filling you with a sense of equilibrium and gratitude. With each sip, visualize your intentions harmonizing within you. Contemplate the gifts of the past season and what you wish to let go of as you prepare for the introspective time of winter. You may use this time to do any additional spell work.

Once you've finished your tea and feel your intentions have been fully honored, express gratitude to the earth, the sun, the elements, and any deities or guides you work with for their support and guidance. Carefully dismantle your grid, cleansing each crystal. These crystals can be kept in your immediate environment or carried with you so they can continue to support your intentions and serve as reminders of your commitment to balance and harmony. Extinguish the candles and remember the blessings of growth and introspection. If possible, offer the tea leaves back to the earth, releasing your past and what you wish to let go.

Samhain Ceremony

Samhain, celebrated from October 31st to November 1st, marks the end of the harvest and the beginning of the darker half of the year. It is a time when the veil between the worlds is at its thinnest, allowing for greater communication with the ancestors and spirits. This ceremony for Samhain can facilitate this connection, honoring the cycle of death and rebirth, and embracing the wisdom of the ancestors.

GRID:

Triple Spiral (the triskelion)

INGREDIENTS AND TOOLS

Crystals

(Sufficient crystals to complete the spirals)

Labradorite

Moonstone

Smoky quartz

Candles

2 black candles

1 white candle

Incense

Mugwort

Sandalwood

Samhain Tea Recipe

1 teaspoon red rooibos

1 teaspoon dried cranberries

1 teaspoon elderberry

¼ teaspoon mugwort

1 teaspoon whole cloves

1 cinnamon stick

Black cloth

Teapot

Cups

RITUAL EXECUTION

Setting the Space

Choose a quiet and sacred space, ideally where you can be undisturbed. Decorate this space with symbols of the season—pumpkins, autumn leaves, skulls, and photos or mementos of passed loved ones to honor the ancestors. Cleanse this space energetically with incense, sound, visualization, or cleansing spray, inviting protective and guiding spirits. Mindfully blend your tea within your teapot, acknowledging its power to open the psychic senses and protect. Boil water as you meditate on the themes of Samhain—reflection, remembrance, and connection to the spiritual realm. Reflect on the cycles of life and the wisdom of the ancestors. With your intentions, program the crystals to connect with the energies of Samhain and your guides.

Grid Layout

Lay your black cloth on the ground or table. In the center, place the teapot as a beacon of spiritual connection and protection, embodying the essence of the thin veil and the spirit world. Begin with the center crystal of the upper spiral, then follow and lay the spiral. Continue with the second spiral and join it at the center. Then lay the third spiral and connect them at the center. As you place each crystal, focus on your intentions to connect with the spiritual realm and honor your ancestors.

Light your candles and incense to honor the elements, the ancestors, and the spirits. The black candle represents protection and the thinning veil, while the white candle represents the guidance and presence of the ancestors. Activate your grid by using the crystal wand, your mind, or your hands to connect each crystal, starting from the first-laid crystal, and using the spaces between the lines to make your way to the heart of the grid. As you do this, visualize your intentions for this ritual. You may vocalize your intentions. Envision the veil thinning and connecting to the crystals. Focus this energy into your teapot and blend. Pour the water over the tea. Let it steep for 5 to 10 minutes. As you steep the tea, visualize opening a channel between you and the spiritual realm, protected and clear. Serve yourself and others the tea. You may also leave out an extra cup as an offering to your ancestors.

Sit comfortably before your crystal tea grid, focusing on the flames and endless spirals of life, death, and rebirth, allowing yourself to feel connected with the spiritual realm and protected. Sip your tea, imagining its essence filling you with clarity and opening a pathway to communicate with the ancestors. With each sip, visualize your intentions reaching through the veil, connecting you with the wisdom of those who came before. Contemplate the cycle of life, the lessons from the past, and the guidance of the ancestors. You may wish to speak aloud the names of those you wish to honor or share stories and memories.

You can write down messages or questions for the ancestors and place them under the smoky quartz, asking for their guidance and wisdom to be revealed to you in dreams or signs. Or you may set out other divination tools to communicate directly.

Once you've finished your tea and feel your intentions have been fully honored, express gratitude to the earth, the elements, the ancestors, and any spirits or deities for their protection and guidance. Carefully dismantle your grid, cleansing each crystal. These crystals can be kept in your environment or carried with you so they can best support your connection to the spiritual realm and act as reminders of the protection and guidance of the ancestors. Extinguish the candles, reflecting on the balance between the worlds and the cycle of life and death. Feel the veil closing gently, leaving you with a sense of peace and connection. If possible, offer the tea leaves back to the earth as an expression of gratitude and completion, and the cup of tea as an offering to the ancestors.

Yule Ceremony

Yule, celebrated on the winter solstice around December 21st, marks the longest night of the year and the rebirth of the sun. It's a time of reflection, renewal, and the return of light. This ceremony for Yule can help to embrace the promise of the returning light, setting intentions for growth, renewal, and the awakening of new dreams.

GRID

Metatron's Cube

INGREDIENTS AND TOOLS

Crystals

1 selenite plate

6 garnet

6 citrine

Candles

3 gold

3 red

Yule Tea Recipe

1 teaspoon black tea

2 teaspoons dried apricot bits

2 teaspoons dried figs

2 teaspoons orange peel

1 dash ground nutmeg

1 cinnamon stick

1 vanilla bean

Gold or white cloth

Teapot

Cups

RITUAL EXECUTION

Setting the Space

Choose a cozy and warm space, ideally where you can be close to nature or have symbols of it. Decorate with evergreens, holly, and candles to symbolize the return of light. Cleanse this space energetically with pine or cedar, visualization, sound bells, or cleansing spray, inviting warmth, light, and renewal. Mindfully blend your tea in a clear bowl and set it aside, acknowledging its properties of renewal and health, embracing their energies of warmth, joy, and abundance. Boil water as you meditate on the themes of Yule—renewal, hope, and the rebirth of the sun. Reflect on what you wish to grow and manifest with the returning light. Set this kettle near your space. With your intentions, program the crystals to connect with the energies of the winter wolstice and the rebirth of the sun.

Grid Layout

Lay your chosen cloth on the ground or table. In the center, lay the selenite plate as a beacon of the sun's returning light and warmth, embodying the essence of Yule. Place a small cloth down, and lay the teapot upon the selenite. Place the six citrine crystals in the inner circle first. Then place the six garnet on the outer circle. Safely surround the grid with the gold and red candles interchangeably. As you place each item, focus on your intentions for renewal, growth, and the awakening of new dreams with the returning light.

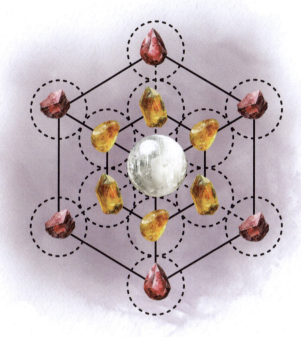

Light your candles to honor the return of the sun and the promise of increasing light. The flames represent the sun's fire, warmth, and life-giving energy. Activate your grid by using the crystal wand, mind, or your hands to connect each crystal, starting from the first-laid crystal. As you do this, visualize your intentions for this ritual. You may vocalize your intentions. Once you sense the shift of energy when this grid is activated, scoop a tablespoon of your tea into the teapot. Focus this energy into your teapot and blend. Pour the water over the tea. Let it steep for 3 to 5 minutes. As you steep the tea, visualize planting the seeds of your intentions, ready to grow with the sun's warmth. Serve yourself and others tea.

Sit comfortably before your crystal tea grid, allowing yourself to feel connected with the sun's energy and the cycle of the year. Sip your tea, imagining its essence filling you with warmth, renewal, and the energy to nurture your intentions. With each sip, visualize the light growing within you, ready to illuminate the path ahead. Contemplate the past year, acknowledging the darkness and challenges faced. Then, shift your focus to the light, recognizing the opportunity for growth, renewal, and the realization of dreams. You may use this time for additional spell work by yourself or with your friends and family.

Once you've finished your tea and feel your intentions have been fully honored, express gratitude to the earth, the sun, the elements, and any deities or guides for their support and the promise of renewal. Carefully dismantle your grid, cleansing each crystal. These crystals can be kept in your environment or carried with you so they can continue to support your intentions and serve as reminders of the light within and the dreams you wish to manifest. Extinguish the candles, reflecting on the return of light and the cycle of growth. Feel the promise of the sun's warmth and energy, even during the longest night.

Elements

Earth Ceremony

Connecting with the energy and element of Earth through this ceremony can be a grounding and nourishing experience, helping to deepen your connection to the natural world, enhance stability in your life, and foster a sense of abundance and well-being, maintaining health, and any kind of long-term gradual workings. This grid may be created and activated at midnight.

GRID

Downward Triangle with line through it

INGREDIENTS AND TOOLS

Crystals

3 moss agate

3 green aventurine

3 red jasper

Candles

2 green

1 brown

Earth Tea Recipe

1 teaspoon roasted barley

Milk

Sugar

Green or brown cloth
Yixing teapot (optional)
Cups

Setting the Space

Choose a location that feels grounding and secure, ideally outdoors on natural ground, but indoors with elements of nature around you can also work. Decorate with natural elements like stones, leaves, branches, and images or symbols of Earth. Cleanse this space energetically with sweetgrass, cleansing spray, or sound, inviting grounding and nurturing energies. Mindfully prepare your tea in your teapot and set it aside, embracing its Earth-connected energies and benefits. Boil water as you meditate on the solidity, richness, and nurturing qualities of Earth. Contemplate how you seek to embody these qualities in your own life. Set this kettle near your space on a wood tray. With your intentions, program the crystals to connect with the energies of the earth.

Grid Layout

Lay your chosen cloth on the ground or table. Lay the three moss agate on each corner of the downward triangle as a beacon of Earth's nurturing and stabilizing energies. Place each red jasper on the triangle lines between the moss agate. Lay the green aventurine across the line crossing through the triangle. As you place each crystal, focus on your intentions to deepen your connection to earth, seeking stability, growth, and protection. Place two green candles on either side of the triangle and the brown candle in the top middle. Set your teapot within the grid.

198

Light your candles to honor the element of Earth and its manifestations in your life—the body, nature, and the physical world around you. Sit comfortably before your crystal tea grid, focusing on the candles and then on the grid, allowing yourself to feel supported and nurtured by Earth. Activate your grid by using the crystal wand, mind, or your hands to connect each crystal, starting from the first-laid crystal. As you do this, visualize your intentions for this ritual. You may vocalize your intentions. Once you sense the shift of energy when this grid is activated, focus this energy into your teapot and tea. Pour the water over the tea. Let it steep for 3 to 5 minutes. As you steep the tea, visualize roots growing from your feet into the ground, connecting you deeply with Earth. Serve yourself and others tea.

Sip your tea, imagining its essence filling you with a sense of stability, nourishment, and a deep connection to the natural world. With each sip, visualize your connection to Earth strengthening, grounding you in the present moment. Reflect on the aspects of your life where you seek more stability, growth, and protection. Contemplate how you can nurture these aspects by embodying the qualities of Earth. You may use this time to do additional Earth-based magick.

Once you've finished your tea and feel your intentions have been fully honored, express gratitude to Earth and the natural world for their constant support, nourishment, and stability. This grid can be left activated for long periods of time. Cleanse and replenish regularly, until it has fulfilled its purpose. Carefully dismantle your grid, cleansing each crystal. These crystals can be kept in your environment where they can best support your connection to Earth or carried with you as reminders of your intentions. Extinguish the candles, reflecting on the deep and nurturing connection you've

cultivated with the earth. Feel grounded and supported, carrying this connection with you in daily life. If possible, offer the tea leaves back to the earth as an expression of gratitude and a symbol of your commitment to nurturing this connection. You may bury them. Remember you may adapt and personalize this ceremony to align with your spiritual path and intentions, embracing the nurturing and grounding energy of Earth.

Air Ceremony

Connecting with the energy of the element Air through this ceremony can enhance communication, creativity, and intellectual clarity while fostering a sense of freedom, lightness, knowledge, and aura replenishment. This ceremony aims to deepen your connection to the mental and spiritual realms, guided by the qualities of Air. This grid may be created and activated at dawn or in the morning.

GRID

Upward Triangle with line through it

INGREDIENTS AND TOOLS

Crystals
3 blue lace agate
3 amethyst
3 clear quartz

Candles
2 light blue
1 white

Air Tea Recipe

Earl Gray tea

Almond milk or cream

Sugar

Blue or white cloth

Glass teapot, cups

RITUAL EXECUTION

Setting the Space

Choose a location that feels open and airy, ideally with natural light or outside where you can feel the breeze. Decorate with feathers, incense, images or symbols of birds, clouds, and the sky to emphasize the Air element. Cleanse this space energetically with oil infuser, visualization, or sound bowls, inviting clarity, inspiration, and the swift movement of air. Mindfully prepare your tea in your teapot and set it aside, embracing its calming, cleansing, and positive energies, acknowledging its properties of mental clarity and freshness. Boil water as you meditate on the qualities of Air—movement, clarity, and freedom of thought and spirit. Set this kettle near your space on a mat. With your intentions, program the crystals to connect with the energies of the Air.

Grid Layout

Lay your chosen cloth on the ground or table. Place the blue lace agate at each corner of the triangle as a beacon of clarity, amplifying your intentions and connecting you to the spiritual realm. Place each clear quartz on the triangle lines between the blue lace agate. Lay the amethyst across the line crossing through the triangle. As you place each crystal, focus on your intentions to enhance communication, creativity, intellectual clarity, and your connection to the spiritual realm. Place two light blue candles on either side of the triangle and the white candle in the top middle. Set your teapot within the grid.

Light your candles to honor the element of Air and its manifestations in your life—thought, communication, and spirituality. Sit comfortably before your crystal tea grid, focusing on the candles and then on the grid with a soft gaze, allowing yourself to connect with the higher realms and the essence of Air. Activate your grid by using a wand, mind, or your hands to connect each crystal, starting from the first-laid crystal. As you do this, visualize your intentions for this ritual. Once you sense the shift of energy when this grid is activated, focus this energy into your teapot and tea. Pour the water over the tea. Let it steep for 3 to 5 minutes. As you steep the tea, visualize your mind becoming as clear and open as the sky. Serve yourself and others tea.

Sip your tea, imagining its essence filling you with mental clarity, creative inspiration, and a sense of calm and openness. With each sip, visualize your connection to the element of Air strengthening, facilitating free-flowing thoughts and ideas. Contemplate the areas of your life where you seek more clarity, creativity, and effective communication. Reflect on how embodying the qualities of Air can support you in achieving these goals. At this point, you may work on any additional Air-based magick.

Once you've finished your tea and feel your intentions have been fully honored, express gratitude to the element of Air for its guidance, inspiration, and the clarity it brings to your life. Carefully dismantle your grid, cleansing each crystal. Extinguish the candles, reflecting on the lightness, freedom, and clarity you've cultivated through your connection with Air. Carry these qualities with you, allowing them to inspire your thoughts and actions in daily life. If possible, offer the tea leaves to the wind as an expression of gratitude to Air, symbolizing your commitment to maintaining this connection and allowing your intentions to be carried by the breeze.

Fire Ceremony

This ceremony will help you connect with the energy and element of Fire, which can ignite passion, enhance transformation, and fuel courage. This ceremony is designed to help you tap into Fire's dynamic and transformative power, fostering personal empowerment, success, and the manifestation of your desires. This grid is ideal for quick and intense workings. This grid may be created and activated at noon.

GRID

Upward Triangle

INGREDIENTS AND TOOLS

Crystals
3 carnelian
3 pyrite

Candles
2 red
1 orange

Fire Tea Recipe

1 teaspoon black tea

¼ teaspoon cinnamon

¼ teaspoon ginger

¼ teaspoon cloves

Red or orange cloth

Cast-iron pot (optional)

Cups

RITUAL EXECUTION

Setting the Space

Choose a location that feels warm and vibrant, perhaps where sunlight streams in or near a fireplace if indoors. Decorate with symbols of Fire, such as candles, images of the sun, volcanoes, or mythical fire creatures like dragons or phoenixes. Cleanse this space energetically with dragon's blood resin, smoke, visualization, or sound bowls, inviting warmth, transformation, and energy. Mindfully prepare your tea in the teapot and set it aside, embracing its fiery, passionate, and vitalizing energies, acknowledging its properties of warmth and stimulation. Boil water as you meditate on the qualities of Fire—transformation, energy, and passion. Set this kettle near your space on a trivet. Program the crystals with your intentions to connect with the energies of the Fire.

Grid Layout

Lay your chosen cloth on the ground or table. Lay the carnelian at each corner of the triangle as a symbol of Fire's energy, amplifying your intentions and protecting against negativity. Place the pyrite upon the lines of the triangle between the carnelian. As you place each crystal, focus on your intentions to ignite passion, enhance transformation, and foster personal empowerment. Place two red candles on either side of the triangle and the orange candle in the top middle. Set your teapot within the grid.

Light your candles to honor the element of Fire and its manifestations in your life—energy, transformation, passion, and power. Sit comfortably before your crystal tea grid, focusing on the candles and the grid, allowing yourself to connect with the essence of Fire. Activate your grid by using a wand, mind, or your hands to connect each crystal, starting from the first-laid crystal. As you do this, visualize your intentions for this ritual. Once you sense the rise in energy when this grid is activated, focus this energy into your teapot and tea. Pour the water over the tea. Let it steep for 3 to 5 minutes. As you steep the tea, visualize your inner fire being kindled, growing in warmth and intensity. Serve yourself and others tea.

Sip your tea, imagining its essence filling you with warmth, courage, and the power to transform and manifest your desires. With each sip, visualize your connection to the element of Fire strengthening, empowering you to act with confidence and vitality. Reflect on the areas of your life where you seek transformation, where you wish to ignite passion, or where you require courage to act. Contemplate how embodying the qualities of Fire can support you in these endeavors. You may wish to write down your reflections or intentions related to your connection with Fire and ignite them in a firesafe bowl for added energy and focus. You may take this time to do additional fire-based magick.

Once you've finished your tea and feel your intentions have been fully honored, express gratitude to the element of Fire for its power, warmth, and transformative energy. Carefully dismantle your grid, cleansing each crystal. These crystals can be kept in your environment where they can best support your connection to Fire or carried with you as reminders of your intentions. Extinguish the candles, reflecting on the dynamic energy and transformative power you've cultivated through your connection with Fire. Carry this power with you, allowing it to inspire action and transformation in your life. If possible, offer the tea leaves as an expression of gratitude to Fire: dry and burn them, symbolizing your commitment to harnessing this element's energy for positive change and personal growth.

Water Ceremony

This ceremony facilitates emotional healing, intuition, and the flow of creativity. This ceremony is designed to help you tap into Water's soothing and reflective properties, encouraging emotional balance, purification, developing psychic abilities, and deeper introspection. This grid may be created and activated at twilight.

GRID

Downward Triangle

INGREDIENTS AND TOOLS

Crystals

3 moonstone

3 aquamarine

Candles

2 blue

1 white

Water Tea Recipe

1 teaspoon chamomile

1 teaspoon blue lotus

1 teaspoon spearmint

1 teaspoon dried apple pieces

Blue or white cloth

Teapot

Cups

RITUAL EXECUTION

Setting the Space

Choose a location that feels calming and reflective, ideally near a body of water like a lake, river, or even a bathtub if indoors. Decorate with symbols of Water such as seashells, images of water landscapes, or representations of aquatic creatures. Cleanse this space energetically with cleansing spray, oil diffuser, or sound bowls, inviting emotional clarity, intuition, and the gentle flow of Water. Mindfully prepare your tea in your teapot and set it aside, embracing its soothing, refreshing, and spiritually connecting energies, acknowledging its properties for calm and emotional healing. Boil water as you consider the qualities of Water—adaptability, depth, and the ability to cleanse and heal. Set this kettle near your space on a mat. With your intentions, program the crystals to connect with the energies of the Water.

Grid Layout

Lay your chosen cloth on the ground or table. Lay the aquamarine at each corner of the triangle, amplifying your intentions and protecting against negativity. Place the moonstone upon the lines of the triangle between the aquamarine. As you place each crystal, focus on your intentions to foster emotional healing, intuition, and the free flow of creativity. Place two blue candles on either side of the triangle and the white candle in the top middle. Set your teapot within the grid.

Light your candles to honor the element of Water and its manifestations in your life—emotions, intuition, and the subconscious mind. Sit comfortably before your crystal tea grid, focusing on the candles and your intention, allowing yourself to connect deeply with the essence of Water. Activate your grid by using a wand, mind, or your hands to connect each crystal, starting from the first-laid crystal. As you do this, visualize your intentions for this ritual. Once you sense the energy is activated, focus this energy into your teapot and tea. Pour the water over the tea. Let it steep for 5 to 10 minutes. As you steep the tea, visualize your emotional state becoming as serene and still as a calm lake. Serve yourself and others tea.

Sip your tea, imagining its essence filling you with tranquility, emotional clarity, and a deeper connection to your intuition. With each sip, visualize your connection to the element of Water strengthening, enabling a flow of creativity and deeper emotional understanding. Reflect on the areas of your life where you seek emotional healing, enhanced intuition, or greater creative expression. Contemplate how embodying the qualities of Water can support you in these endeavors. You may begin to do other Water-based magick within the grid.

Once you've finished your tea and feel your intentions have been fully honored, express gratitude to the element of Water for its healing, intuition, and creative flow. Carefully dismantle your grid, cleansing each crystal. Extinguish the candles, reflecting on the emotional balance, intuitive insights, and creative inspirations you've cultivated through your connection with Water. Carry these qualities with you, allowing them to guide and soothe you in daily life. If possible, offer the tea leaves back to a body of water or the earth as an expression of gratitude to Water, symbolizing your commitment to maintaining this elemental balance and harmony. You may make a weaker brew and water your garden.

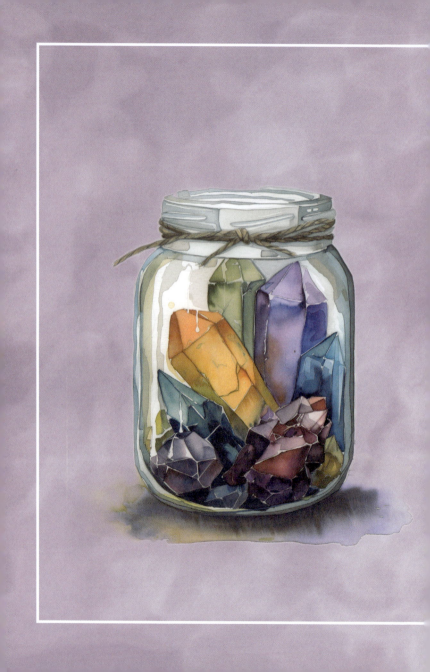

Crystal Elixirs for Magickal Intent

rystal elixirs, also known as gem waters or crystal-infused waters, are a form of alternative medicine or magickal potion that involve immersing crystals in water to imbue the water with the vibrational energies of the crystals. I have found that drinking this water transfers the healing properties of the crystals to the body, promoting physical, emotional, and spiritual well-being. The process of creating a crystal elixir generally involves selecting tumbled crystals based on their corresponding properties (see Appendix B). They are then cleansed and gently cleaned and placed in water to charge for a period of time. It's important to note that not all crystals are safe to place directly in water due to their chemical composition or potential toxicity. Therefore, some practitioners use an indirect method, where the crystal is placed adjacent to, but not directly in, the water. This method also preserves the integrity of the crystal from degrading over time. This will serve the same purpose with the same vibrational effects. Of course, always remember that crystals are not to be consumed internally, as this can be dangerous. Always handle your elixirs and health mindfully.

While you can use only crystals for your elixirs, you have the freedom to explore and have fun mixing in herbs to your concoctions! You may also use your elixirs as body sprays, room sprays, and for your bath. If you decide to use it primarily for this, you may also add essential oils for external purposes.

The Direct Method

Select a crystal that connects to your specific needs. Cleanse the crystal by holding it under running water and visualize white light washing over it. All negative and old energies will simply wash away. (If you are handling crystals that absolutely cannot get wet, choose another method to cleanse them.) Place your crystal in a glass vessel and pour spring or distilled water over it. Leave the vessel out in the sun to receive solar energy or under the moonlight for lunar energy (new moon); let sit for 12 to 24 hours. If the crystal is one that cannot be left submerged for long periods of time—such as jasper, citrine, or carnelian—you can cut this time frame down depending on the stone. Strain the liquid directly into a large glass bottle using a tea or coffee filter to get rid of any possible debris. Fill the bottle until it is two-thirds full of the elixir, then add one-third vodka or brandy as a preservative. You may substitute vegetable glycerin instead of alcohol. This will sanitize the crystal elixir and prevent contamination over time. The final formulation should be approximately 70 percent elixir water and 30 percent alcohol. Label and date this large bottle as the "Mother" elixir, indicating the elixir by recipe name so that you know what crystals you used. If you plan on simply drinking the elixir right then and there, you can skip this preservative step. Otherwise, you may simply add a dozen drops to a glass of fresh water and enjoy.

You may also fill a smaller glass dropper bottle with pure water, and add a dozen drops of the "Mother" elixir. This allows you to have a travel-sized elixir to use throughout the day. Despite it containing only a small amount of the "Mother," it is enough for the vibrational energies to transfer over to the new vessel.

The Indirect Method

I enjoy and prefer this method most; I still gain the same benefits, but it takes out the risk of any toxicity or debris, and protects the structure of my crystals. Plus, it leaves more room to choose from a variety of crystals, even the ones that cannot get wet. Nevertheless, whenever you create your own recipes, always research to confirm that your chosen crystal does not contain harmful elements that could leach out into water, even with the indirect method.

If you are using anything other than quartz, you must place these crystals in an empty small glass jar, then place that within another larger glass bowl. Fill the bowl (not the smaller jar) with spring or distilled water, and, as with the direct method, set it outdoors to infuse either in the sun (if compatible) or moon. From here, follow the same steps to create the "Mother" elixir to preserve.

Water-Safe Crystals

The following crystals are those most ideal for crystal elixirs, as they are safe to use near or in water. Remember: you are merely taking in the energies of the crystals—*please do not actually consume them.* Use them only with intention and for their healing frequencies.

AGATE

The good-luck stone. This crystal offers protection and strength, and enhances mental concentration and wisdom. It naturally balances the yin/yang energy and rebalances the mind, body, and soul. It is an ideal stone for opening and connecting to the solar plexus and crown chakras. It stimulates good health, pleasure, joy, and happiness. It's the most ideal gem to help free others from any bitterness they may be harboring, helping them come to terms with forgiveness and showing compassion. This is also the perfect stone to protect you from anything that may drain you mentally, emotionally, or spiritually.

AMETHYST

The ultimate spiritual, meditative, and calming crystal. It increases intuition and psychic powers, encourages mental and emotional stability, strength, and inner peace, and helps you cope with loss or change. It's the perfect crystal to promote restful sleep, ease head tension, and support general healing and the immune system. It lends high vibrations to the third-eye and crown chakras.

AVENTURINE

The stone of prosperity. This crystal promotes leadership qualities, compassion, and empathy. It calms frustration, soothes anger, and protects against hasty decisions and rash responses. It delivers vitality, wisdom, and growth; it helps attract hope, joy, change, prosperity, and good fortune. It aids the circulatory system and the general well-being of the heart, making it the most ideal for the heart chakra.

BLACK OBSIDIAN

The breaker-of-chains stone. This stone is ideal for absorbing negativity and cutting emotional cords that block and inhibit growth, positivity, and the ability to move on. It aids in deflecting bad magick and any negative spells or entities that feed on energy. Clears the auric field, helps with self-control, and heals shock and trauma. Rebalances the digestive system, relieves joint pain, and releases addictions and bad habits. May also be used to protect and bring out the truth, shatter illusions, and remove blockages. Stimulates and raises the root chakra.

CARNELIAN

The vitality stone. This crystal has long been used in healing and in restoring vitality, creativity, and inspiration to the bearer. It brings warm, joyous, and courageous vibrations. Mentally, it anchors people to the present while emotionally helping them accept and understand what it is that they need to cope with. It stimulates the circulatory,

digestive, reproductive, and muscular systems. It balances and opens the sacral and solar plexus chakras, thus making it an ideal stone for inspiring passion and sexuality.

CITRINE

The crystal of success. This gem is the perfect stone to draw success, prosperity, and abundance, especially in business or money matters. It also promotes wisdom, joy, and intellect, making it the most ideal stone to clear your mind and easily tune in to the advice of the inner voice. It also dispels negative thoughts. It is rich with positive energies, making it a good companion to inspire and to keep one constantly motivated. Aids in bringing power and energy to the solar plexus chakra.

CLEAR QUARTZ

Clear quartz is a universal crystal that can be used in all your tea witchery. It is a master healer and amplifies whatever energy is within your intentions. It absorbs, stores, reflects, amplifies, balances, and focuses energy. It balances the emotions and promotes a healthy immune system. Clear quartz aligns all the chakras (it specifically represents the crown chakra), and therefore also balances your spellwork.

JASPER

The stone of protection. This crystal balances the energies—the yin/yang—making it a good grounding stone. It promotes mental clarity and focus, calms the senses, and allows the receiver to relax and organize their thoughts. It could possibly heal the reproductive system and deliver strength and vitality. Jasper harmonizes the mind, body, and soul, helping to protect against illness and disease. Depending upon the color of the stone (jasper can range from red to yellow to green), it can be associated with different chakra points, but it is most often connected to the root and sacral chakras.

MOONSTONE

The stone of new beginnings. These crystals have always been deeply associated with the energies of the moon and with moon deities. Moonstone enhances and helps develop psychic abilities, intuition, and clairvoyance. It is believed to heal conditions connected to the reproductive system, hormones, especially for conception, pregnancy, and childbirth. It soothes emotional and spiritual imbalances and stress, and may also be used to cleanse karmic pain passed down generationally. It raises the vibrations of the third eye, throat, and crown chakras.

ROSE QUARTZ

 Rose quartz is the stone of gentleness; it is known as the stone of the heart. It inspires and promotes love and beauty and expands these vibrations to the self and the environment, as well as to the universe, making it the perfect crystal for petitions to the guiding spirits and deities. An ideal gem to have upon a tea altar dedicated to a god or goddess or the ancestors. It has a powerful effect on the heart and emotions and is associated with the heart chakra. This gem is best for soothing tempers, asking forgiveness, and inspiring love and passion.

SMOKEY QUARTZ

 The grounding stone. An excellent gem to combat negative emotions and protect from stressful vibrations and nightmares. It brings clarity of mind and helps bring balance during meditations and psychic work. These crystals are ideal to aid in magick where you want to change bad moods to good, or to banish negative feelings and replace them with positive ones. An ideal stone for protection and to prepare the body for astral projection during sleep. This crystal will always help bring a person back to reality. It protects against bad influences and negative materialistic affairs, and is a good crystal for business and finances. It brings grounding vibrations to the root chakra.

TIGER'S EYE

The crystal of confidence. This gem inspires higher self-esteem. It boosts the ability to overcome inner struggles and life's difficulties by soothing and bringing emotional balance and clarity. It strengthens mental willpower and brings protection and luck. It motivates the bearer to go with the flow and overcome fears, increasing peace and relaxation. It is associated with the sacral and solar plexus chakras.

Recipes

These eleven crystal elixir recipes are designed for some of the most common everyday intentions. While I have found these recipes to be ideal for the described outcomes, please bear in mind that they serve as a guide. Trust your intuition and mix and match for your own needs, desires, and preferences, always keeping your health front of mind. To ensure absolute safety, use the indirect method for all these elixirs, especially if you're not certain about their water safety.

Serenity Elixir

Intention: Calmness and peace

Crystal: Blue lace agate, amethyst, rose quartz

Suggested Herbs: Lavender, peppermint

INSTRUCTIONS

Gather the cleansed crystals in a small glass jar. Place this jar in a larger bowl of spring or distilled water. You may place the suggested herbs within the larger bowl of water. Let it rest under the moonlight overnight to imbue calmness and to help with any anxieties. Use this elixir to soothe emotions and bring peace.

Focus Elixir

Intention: Concentration and clarity

Crystal: Fluorite, clear quartz, citrine

Suggested Herbs: Mint, lemon verbena

Gather the cleansed crystals in a small glass jar. Place this jar in a larger bowl of spring or distilled water. You may place the suggested herbs within the larger bowl of water. This elixir should be made in the morning, to allow it to charge in gentle morning sunlight for a few hours. Drink to enhance focus and mental clarity.

Vitality Elixir

Intention: Energy and vitality

Crystal: Carnelian, clear quartz, agate

Suggested Herbs: Cinnamon sticks, ginger root, chrysanthemum

INSTRUCTIONS

Gather the cleansed crystals in a small glass jar. Place this jar in a larger bowl of spring or distilled water. You may place the suggested herbs within the larger bowl of water. Leave in sunlight for 3 to 4 hours to energize. Sip for a boost in vitality and motivation.

Healing Elixir

Intention: Healing and abundance

Crystal: Jade, rose quartz, agate

Suggested Herbs: Thyme, marjoram, saffron

Gather the cleansed crystals in a small glass jar. Place this jar in a larger bowl of spring or distilled water. You may place the suggested herbs within the larger bowl of water. Let it sit in a patch of grass or under a green leafy tree for the day. Use this elixir to encourage healing and attract abundance.

Sleep Elixir

Intention: Better sleep and dreams

Crystal: Amethyst, rose quartz, smoky quartz

Suggested Herbs: Valerian, elderflower, lavender

INSTRUCTIONS

Gather the cleansed crystals in a small glass jar. Place this jar in a larger bowl of spring or distilled water. You may place the suggested herbs within the larger bowl of water. Let it charge under the stars overnight. Drink before bedtime to promote restful sleep and insightful dreams.

Love Elixir

Intention: Love and harmony

Crystal: Rose quartz, rhodonite, clear quartz

Suggested Herbs: Rose, hibiscus, geranium

INSTRUCTIONS

Gather the cleansed crystals in a small glass jar. Place this jar in a larger bowl of spring or distilled water. You may place the suggested herbs within the larger bowl of water. Allow it to charge in the early morning sunlight. Consume to open the heart to love and harmony.

Protection Elixir

Intention: Protection and grounding

Crystal: Black obsidian, red jasper, smoky quartz

Suggested Herbs: Basil, rosemary, cinnamon stick

INSTRUCTIONS

Gather the cleansed crystals in a small glass jar. Place this jar in a larger bowl of spring or distilled water. You may place the suggested herbs within the larger bowl of water. Let it charge away from direct light, in a secure dark space or altar. Drink for grounding and to ward off negativity.

Intuition Elixir

Intention: Intuition and feminine energy

Crystal: Moonstone, amethyst, clear quartz

Suggested Herbs: Mugwort, cloves, lavender

INSTRUCTIONS

Gather the cleansed crystals in a small glass jar. Place this jar in a larger bowl of spring or distilled water. You may place the suggested herbs within the larger bowl of water. Let it bask in the light of the full moon. Use this elixir to enhance intuition and connect with feminine energies.

Creativity Elixir

Intention: Creativity and playfulness

Crystal: Orange calcite, carnelian, clear quartz

Suggested Herbs: Basil, coriander, lavender

INSTRUCTIONS

Gather the cleansed crystals in a small glass jar. Place this jar in a larger bowl of spring or distilled water. You may place the suggested herbs within the larger bowl of water. Place in a sunny spot to imbue it with vibrant, creative energies. Sip to inspire creativity and joy.

Wealth Elixir

Intention: Wealth and success

Crystal: Pyrite, aventurine, citrine

Suggested Herbs: Basil, bergamot, ginger

INSTRUCTIONS

Gather the cleansed crystals in a small glass jar. Place this jar in a larger bowl of spring or distilled water. You may place the suggested herbs within the larger bowl of water. Let it charge in bright sunlight for a few hours. Drink to attract wealth, abundance, and success.

Seven Sisters Elixir

Intention: Healing, spiritual growth, purification, chakra balancing, psychic enhancement, protection, connecting to the higher realms and Mother Earth.

Crystals: Amethyst, clear quartz, smoky quartz, cacoxenite, rutile, goethite, lepidocrocite

Suggested Herbs: Chamomile, lavender, peppermint, holy basil (tulsi), rosemary, lemon balm, sage

INSTRUCTIONS

Gather the cleansed crystals in a small glass jar. Place this jar in a larger bowl of spring or distilled water. You may place the suggested herbs within the larger bowl of water. Let it charge during either a solar eclipse or the Taurid meteor shower. This elixir provides powerful healing and spiritual benefits that can help clear, balance, and enhance the energies of those who drink it.

Tea Blends for Daily Health

These tea blends have been crafted by combining various herbs, spices, and tea leaves to target particular health issues and promote general daily wellness. Each ingredient is chosen for its unique therapeutic properties, and when combined, they work to enhance the desired healing effect. While these tea blends can offer health benefits and support well-being, it's important to approach them as complementary remedies rather than replacements for conventional medical treatment. The efficacy of these teas can vary from person to person, and some herbs may interact with medications or be unsuitable for certain health conditions. Consulting with a healthcare provider before incorporating therapeutic tea blends into your routine is advisable, especially if you are pregnant, nursing, or taking medication.

Digestive Tea

This tea can help soothe stomach issues and aid digestion. It's beneficial in reducing nausea and can help with bloating and gas. Keep in mind that this blend does contain caffeine.

INGREDIENTS

1 part green tea

1 part peppermint

1 part chamomile

1 part ginger root (dried or fresh)

½ part fennel seeds

Optional: ¼ part licorice root (for sweetness and additional digestive support, but avoid if you have high blood pressure)

INSTRUCTIONS

Combine all the dried herbs in a bowl. If you're using fresh ginger, it's best to add it directly to the tea while brewing rather than mixing it with the dried herbs. Transfer the blend to an airtight container, and store it in a cool, dry place to maintain freshness.

For a single cup, use 1 to 2 teaspoons of the tea blend per cup of boiling water. If using fresh ginger, add a ½ inch slice (or to taste) directly into the pot or mug. Pour boiling water over the herbs (and fresh ginger, if using), and allow to steep covered for 5 to 10 minutes. The longer it steeps, the more potent the effects, but also the stronger the flavor. Strain the tea. You can add a teaspoon of honey for sweetness if desired.

Enjoy a cup of this digestive tea after meals to aid digestion or whenever you're experiencing digestive discomfort.

Relaxation Tea

This calming and mood soothing blend helps reduce stress and anxiety. It is especially ideal to drink at the end of the day, before bed.

INGREDIENTS

1 part chamomile

1 part passionflower

1 part lemon balm

½ part peppermint

Optional: ¼ part valerian root (use sparingly)

INSTRUCTIONS

Gently mix all the dried herbs together in a bowl. If you're sensitive to any of the herbs or prefer a different taste, feel free to adjust the proportions. If you're using valerian root, make sure to include it as part of the mix. Transfer the blend to an airtight container and store it in a cool, dry place away from direct sunlight to preserve its aromatic and medicinal qualities.

For a single serving, use 1 to 2 teaspoons of the tea blend per cup (8 oz.) of boiling water. Pour the boiling water over the herbs in a teapot or a cup. Cover and steep for 5 to 10 minutes. The longer it steeps, the more potent the flavors and effects.

Strain the tea into a cup. You can add a natural sweetener like honey or stevia if desired, but often the natural flavors are delightful on their own. Sip this tea in the evening or anytime you wish to relax and unwind. Its calming effects are perfect for preparing for meditation, winding down before bedtime, or simply taking a quiet moment for yourself.

If you choose to include valerian root, be aware that it has a very strong, somewhat earthy taste that not everyone enjoys. Start with a small amount and adjust according to your taste and the effects.

Immune-Boosting Tea

This blend is ideal to help increase the body's resistance to infection. It provides a great boost of antioxidants and vitamins, and also has antiinflammatory properties that will help with your digestion and respiratory health.

INGREDIENTS:

1 part echinacea
1 part elderberry
1 part ginger root
½ part licorice root
½ part peppermint
Optional: A pinch of cayenne pepper for an extra kick
and to further stimulate the immune system

INSTRUCTIONS

Combine all the dried herbs in a bowl. If you're using fresh ginger, it's best to grate a small amount directly into your cup when brewing, rather than mixing it into the herb blend. Transfer the blend to an airtight container, storing it in a cool, dry place to maintain its potency.

For a single cup, use 1 to 2 teaspoons of the tea blend per cup (8 oz.) of boiling water. If adding fresh ginger or cayenne pepper, do so according to your taste preference at this time. Pour boiling water over the blend and allow it to steep covered for 10 to 15 minutes. Covering the tea helps to ensure that the volatile oils and beneficial properties of the herbs are retained.

Strain the tea to remove the herbs. You can add a teaspoon of honey and lemon juice, especially if you're dealing with a sore throat or cough, as honey has soothing and antimicrobial properties. Enjoy 1 to 2 cups a day, especially during cold and flu season, to help boost your immune system.

Licorice root should be used cautiously, especially by those with high blood pressure or kidney disease, or who are pregnant. It can be omitted from the blend if necessary.

Detox Tea

This rich antioxidant and antiinflammatory blend will help aid in the detoxification and regeneration of the liver, blood, and kidneys.

INGREDIENTS

1 part dandelion root
1 part milk thistle seed
1 part nettle leaf
½ part burdock root
½ part peppermint

Optional: A pinch of turmeric root powder for its antiinflammatory properties and support of liver function

INSTRUCTIONS

Gently mix all the dried ingredients in a bowl. Ensure that any larger pieces, like dandelion or burdock root, are finely chopped or ground to ensure even infusion. Transfer the blend to an airtight container. Store in a cool, dry place away from direct sunlight to preserve the blend's efficacy.

Use 1 to 2 teaspoons of the tea blend per cup (8 oz.) of boiling water. Pour boiling water over the herbs in a teapot or a cup. Cover and allow to steep for 10 to 15 minutes. Covering the tea while it steeps helps to retain the volatile oils and full benefits of the herbs.

Strain the tea to remove the solid materials. If you wish, you can sweeten the tea with a small amount of honey or enjoy it as is to appreciate the natural flavors. Drink a cup of this detox tea blend in the morning or before bed. It's best to start with one cup a day to see how your body responds before increasing to two cups.

Always consult with a healthcare provider before starting any detox regimen, especially if you have existing health conditions or are taking medications, as some herbs can interact with medications. Drinking plenty of water is crucial when using detoxifying herbs to help flush toxins from the body. Pay attention to your body's responses. Detox teas can be powerful, and it's essential to ensure they suit your individual health needs.

Energy-Boosting Tea

This tea blend is made to help improve brain function and energy levels. It brings a balancing boost of energy that can help increase mental focus and physical endurance, and help diminish fatigue. Keep in mind that this blend does contain caffeine.

INGREDIENTS

1 part green tea
1 part yerba maté
1 part ginseng root
½ part peppermint
½ part lemongrass

Optional: A pinch of cayenne pepper to stimulate circulation and metabolism, further enhancing the energizing effect

INSTRUCTIONS

Carefully mix all the dried ingredients in a bowl to ensure an even distribution. For the ginseng root, ensure it's finely chopped or ground for optimal infusion. Transfer your blend to an airtight container. Keep it in a cool, dry place away from direct sunlight to preserve its potency and freshness.

Use 1 to 2 teaspoons of the tea blend per cup (8 oz.) of boiling water. Boil water to 175F. Pour the hot water over the tea blend in a teapot or a cup. Cover and steep for 3 to 5 minutes. Strain the tea to remove the leaves and optional roots. If desired, you can add a teaspoon of honey for sweetness or a slice of lemon for extra zest and vitamin C, which can also enhance energy levels.

Enjoy a cup of this energy-boosting tea blend in the morning or early afternoon to invigorate your day. Avoid drinking it late in the evening to prevent any interference with sleep.

Embracing the Path of Harmony

The magickal practice of tea and crystals is a path not merely about learning techniques or collecting beautiful crystals and herbs; it is a profound journey of self-discovery, transformation, and alignment with the universe and Mother Nature's energies. I find it often essential to pause and reflect on the journey that has been undertaken.

Reflection is a powerful tool on this path. It allows us to see how far we have come, to recognize the shifts within us, and to acknowledge the lessons we have learned. Every cup of tea brewed with intention and every crystal grid created is a step on your journey of personal transformation. Remember to honor and embrace the changes within you and let them guide you toward a deeper understanding of yourself and the magick that is a part of you.

Balance and mindfulness have always been cornerstones of making this a fulfilling practice. When pursuing the path toward spiritual growth, it is all too easy to get caught up in seeking profound experiences or dramatic shifts. It's important to reflect that the true essence of this path lies in the balance between action and reflection, giving and receiving, moving forward and pausing to be present. Mindfulness is the true art of being fully present in the moment—it will enrich your practice by allowing you to experience the full depth of each ritual, each cup of tea, and each crystal's energy.

Manifestation is a powerful aspect of this magickal practice, yet it requires clarity, intention, and alignment with our highest good. Let your intentions be guided by your true self, and not by fleeting desires or external pressures. Trust in the wisdom of the universe and know that what is meant for you will come to you with perfect timing.

As you continue your path, remember that the journey itself is the destination. Each step, each discovery, and each challenge are a part of your spiritual evolution. Be gentle with yourself, and know that it is okay to rest, to reassess, and to redirect your path as needed. Tea is always the best tool to take that much-needed break.

Keep your heart and mind open to the lessons and messages that come your way. The universe, with its infinite wisdom and love, is always guiding and supporting you; your own inner truth and power will always connect you to the infinite possibilities and strength to move ever forward.

As you continue your tea practice, remember these helpful words: *Stay Curious.* Stay curious and open to learning new things about tea, crystals, and, most importantly, yourself. Create your own personal rituals that anchor your practice in your daily life; make them a living, breathing part of your existence. Connect with community. Tea must be shared! Share your journey with others who walk similar paths— the trusted tea circles you find and build upon will always heal and embrace you. Sustain your connection to nature for it is the ultimate source of energy and inspiration. Remember that both tea and crystals are gifts from the earth. Let the magickal practice of tea and crystals be a source of light, guidance, and transformation on your journey. May it bring you closer to your true self, help you manifest your deepest desires, and instill a sense of peace and harmony within your soul. Walk your path with wisdom and grace, knowing that each step is a part of the beautiful tapestry of your life's journey.

Great Blessings!

Acknowledgments

I am blessed to have so many people in my life who support and encourage my writing. First, I'd like to thank my husband and my son: they have always been my greatest motivators and team throughout my writing journey, and I couldn't have asked for a better life together. Many long nights my husband stepped up and provided us with meals and comfort. I'm grateful for my son's amazing patience and ever joyful personality. Their ongoing love and support always leave me speechless and help me to keep my vision and writing alive. Thank you to my parents for giving me the freedom to find myself and my path, for always encouraging me to pursue my passions and share my knowledge.

I'm also thankful to my community of friends, who have become my greatest circle. Words cannot express how truly lucky I feel for having found you all. You are my greatest inspiration. To the Witches of Hemet, you were my beginning and the beat to my heart. Each of you brought me healing and experiences I will never forget. Thank you for giving me the honor in being your HP. To the Pagan community of the Alabama River Region, you have become more than friends to me. You are my circle of wisdom, strength, hope, and support. We have learned so much by sharing with each other; I thank you for this grace.

I would like to thank the entire team at Red Wheel/Weiser for making my books possible. You saw great potential in *A Tea Witch's Grimoire* and gave me the foundation and platform to share my energy and knowledge with the world. Thank you Judika Illes and Kathryn Sky-Peck for your editorial and design support and for nurturing my work—it is far better than it would be without you. I am honored to have you all.

Herb Correspondences:
Magickal Goals and Intentions

ASTRAL PROJECTION

caraway

dandelion

fennel

hibiscus

marjoram

mugwort

parsley

BEAUTY

catnip

ginseng, American

CHASTITY

coconut

cucumber

hawthorn

lavender

pineapple

vervain

COURAGE

basil

black tea

borage

cohosh, black

ginger

mullein

nettle

pepper

rooibos

thyme

yarrow

DIVINATION

cherry

dandelion

fig

goldenrod

hibiscus

lemongrass

marjoram

oolong tea

orange

pomegranate

EXORCISM

American elder

angelica

basil

black tea

clove
clover
cumin
garlic
horehound
juniper
lemon
lemongrass
lilac
mallow
milk thistle
mint
mullein
nettle
onion
orange bergamot
peach
pepper
pine nut
rosemary
yarrow

FERTILITY
banana
carrot
cinnamon
coriander
cucumber
fig

geranium
grape
hawthorn
hazelnut
mint
mustard
nuts
palm, date
peach
pine nut
pomegranate
rice
tea, white

FIDELITY
American elder
American skullcap
chickweed
chili pepper
clover
cumin
licorice
nutmeg
yerba maté

FRIENDSHIPS
lemon
oolong tea
passionflower

GOSSIP—TO HALT
clove

HAPPINESS
catnip

cinnamon

feverfew

hawthorn

lavender

marjoram

mint

saffron

thyme

vanilla

white tea

HEALING—TO PROMOTE
allspice

almond

American elder

American ginseng

angelica

apple

barley

bay

blackberry

chamomile

cinnamon

citron

cucumber

fennel

garlic

green tea

hemp

hops

horehound

lemon balm

lime

milk thistle

mint

mugwort

nettle

onion

orange bergamot

pepper

peppermint

plum

potato

rose

rosemary

saffron

sorrel

spearmint

thyme

vervain

violet

willow

HEALTH—TO MAINTAIN
allspice
angelica
caraway
cinnamon
chamomile
coriander
galangal
geranium
juniper
marjoram
mullein
nutmeg
oats
orange bergamot
sorrel
thyme
walnut

HEXES—TO BREAK
chili pepper
galangal
lemongrass
milk thistle
orange bergamot
vetiver

IMMORTALITY
apple
chrysanthemum

green tea
linden
sage

LONGEVITY
green tea
lavender
lemon
maple
peach
sage

LOVE
American ginseng
American skullcap
apple
apricot
bachelor's button
barley
basil
black cohosh
Brazil nut
cardamom
catnip
chamomile
cherry
chestnut
chickweed
chili pepper
cinnamon

clove

clover

coriander

damiana

dill

elecampane

fig

geranium

ginger

hemp

hibiscus

jasmine

juniper

lavender

lemon

lemon balm

lemon verbena

licorice

lime

linden

lovage

mallow

maple

marjoram

nuts

orange

papaya

peach

pear

peppermint

plum

raspberry

rose

rosemary

saffron

spearmint

strawberry

sugarcane

tea

thyme

tormentil

valerian

vanilla

vervain

vetiver

violet

willow

wormwood

yarrow

yerba maté

LOVE DIVINATION

mullein

rose

willow

LOVE SPELLS—TO BREAK

pistachio

LUCK

allspice
almond
chamomile
hazelnut
honeysuckle
linden
nutmeg
orange
pineapple
pomegranate
rose
star anise
strawberry
vanilla
vetiver
violet

LUST—TO DECREASE

vervain

LUST—TO INCREASE

American ginseng
caraway
cardamom
carrot
celery
cinnamon
damiana
dill

galangal
garlic
ginger
hibiscus
lemongrass
licorice
lemon leaf
mint
nettle
onion
parsley
rosemary
saffron
tea, green
vanilla
violet
yerba maté

MENTAL POWERS—TO STRENGTHEN

caraway
celery
ginger
grape
horehound
lemongrass
marjoram
orange
peppermint
rooibos

rosemary

spearmint

summer savory

tea

walnut

MONEY

allspice

almond

American elder

basil

black tea

blackberry

buckwheat

cashew

chamomile

cinnamon

cinquefoil

clove

clover

dill

fenugreek

galangal

ginger

goldenrod

grape

honeysuckle

jasmine

maple

marjoram

mint

nutmeg

oats

onion

orange

orange bergamot

pecan

pineapple

pomegranate

rice

spearmint

vanilla

vervain

vetiver

woodruff

PEACE

American skullcap

lavender

lemon balm

marjoram

mint

passionflower

sage

thyme

vervain

violet

POWER

ginger

lemongrass

tea

PROPHETIC DREAMS

cinquefoil

dandelion

hibiscus

jasmine

lemongrass

marigold

mugwort

onion

rose

PROSPERITY

almond

banana

chamomile

cinnamon

ginger

honeysuckle

nuts

oats

vanilla

PROTECTION

agrimony

American elder

American ginseng

angelica

anise

barley

basil

bay

black cohosh

blackberry

blueberry

caraway

chrysanthemum

cinnamon

cinquefoil

clove

clover

coconut

cumin

dill

elecampane

fennel

galangal

garlic

geranium

hazelnut

honeysuckle

horehound

hyssop

juniper

lavender

lilac

lime

linden

mallow

marigold

marjoram

mint

milk thistle

mugwort

mullein

nettle

onion

orange bergamot

papaya

parsley

pepper

peppermint

plum

raspberry

rice

rose

rosemary

sage

tormentil

valerian

vervain

violet

white tea

willow

woodruff

wormwood

PSYCHIC POWERS

acacia

bay

borage

celery

cinnamon

citron

elecampane

galangal

honeysuckle

lemongrass

marigold

marjoram

mugwort

orange

peppermint

rose

saffron

star anise

thyme

wormwood

yarrow

PURIFICATION

acacia

anise

bay

chamomile
coconut
fennel
hyssop
lavender
lemon
lemongrass
lemon verbena
milk thistle
parsley
peppermint
rosemary
sugarcane
tea
thyme
turmeric
valerian
vervain

SLEEP

agrimony
American elder
chamomile
cinquefoil
elder, American
hops
lavender
linden
passionflower

peppermint
rosemary
thyme
valerian
vervain

SPIRITS—TO CALL

dandelion
milk thistle
pu-erh tea
wormwood

SPIRITUALITY

acacia
cinnamon
ginger
tea

STRENGTH

bay
black tea
milk thistle
mugwort
rooibos
saffron

SUCCESS

almond
bay
chamomile
cinnamon

clover
ginger
honeysuckle
lemon balm
marjoram
rosemary
saffron
vanilla

VISIONS
angelica
damiana
lemongrass

WISDOM
almond
chamomile
dill
ginger

peach
peppermint
rooibos
sage
tea

WISHES
American ginseng
dandelion
hazelnut
pomegranate
sage
violet
walnut

YOUTH—TO MAINTAIN
anise
rosemary
vervain

Crystal Correspondences:
Magickal Goals and Intentions

ASTRAL PROJECTION

amethyst

black tourmaline

clear quartz

labradorite

lapis lazuli

moonstone

selenite

BEAUTY

amethyst

aquamarine

citrine

clear quartz

jade

moonstone

rose quartz

CHASTITY

agate

amethyst

black tourmaline

clear quartz

garnet

moonstone

sapphire

COURAGE

amethyst

aquamarine

black tourmaline

bloodstone

carnelian

lapis lazuli

red jasper

tiger's eye

DIVINATION

amethyst

black obsidian

clear quartz

fluorite

labradorite

lapis lazuli

moonstone

selenite

EXORCISM

amethyst

black obsidian

black tourmaline
hematite
labradorite
lodolite
selenite
smoky quartz

FERTILITY

carnelian
green aventurine
moonstone
rhodonite
rose quartz
ruby zoisite
shiva lingam
unakite

FIDELITY

amethyst
blue sapphire
emerald
garnet
jade
lapis lazuli
rhodochrosite
ruby

FRIENDSHIP

amazonite
amethyst

aquamarine
citrine
garnet
green aventurine
lapis lazuli
larimar
rhodochrosite
rhodonite
rose quartz
selenite
spirit quartz
sugilite
turquoise

GOSSIP—TO HALT

amethyst
aquamarine
black tourmaline
blue lace agate
chrysocolla
sodalite
tiger's eye

HAPPINESS

amethyst
aventurine
carnelian
citrine
jade

rose quartz
sodalite
sunstone

HEALING—TO PROMOTE

amethyst
black tourmaline
bloodstone
citrine
clear quartz
emerald
golden healer
jade
lapis lazuli
rose quartz
selenite
turquoise

HEALTH—TO MAINTAIN

amethyst
bloodstone
citrine
clear quartz
garnet
green aventurine
jade
shungite
sodalite
turquoise

HEXES—TO BREAK

amethyst
black tourmaline
clear quartz
fire agate
hematite
jet
labradorite
obsidian
selenite
smoky quartz

IMMORTALITY

amethyst
aquamarine
clear quartz
garnet
jade
lapis lazuli
moldavite
serpentine
shungite
turquoise

LONGEVITY

amethyst
bloodstone
citrine
clear quartz
garnet

lapis lazuli

serpentine

shungite jade

turquoise

LOVE

amazonite

amethyst

emerald

garnet

green aventurine

kunzite

lapis lazuli

larimar

moonstone

pink opal

rhodochrosite

rhodonite

rose quartz

selenite

spirit quartz

sugilite

LOVE DIVINATION

amethyst

clear quartz

garnet

kunzite

lapis lazuli

malachite

moonstone

pink opal

rhodonite

rose quartz

LOVE SPELLS—TO BREAK

amethyst

black obsidian

black tourmaline

clear quartz

hematite

labradorite

obsidian

selenite

smoky quartz

LUCK

amethyst

carnelian

citrine

garnet

green aventurine

jade

labradorite

peridot

pyrite

tiger's eye

LUST—TO DECREASE

amethyst

black tourmaline

blue lace agate

chrysoprase

garnet

hematite

lepidolite

shungite

sodalite

tiger's eye

LUST—TO INCREASE

carnelian

garnet

moonstone

red jasper

rhodonite

rose quartz

ruby

serpentine

sunstone

tiger's eye

MENTAL POWERS—TO STRENGTHEN

amethyst

apophyllite

azurite

blue or green kyanite

citrine

clear quartz

fluorite

hematite

labradorite

lapis lazuli

larimar

pyrite

selenite

sodalite

tiger's eye

MONEY

black tourmaline

citrine

green aventurine

green jade

malachite

moss agate

peridot

pyrite

ruby

tiger's eye

PEACE

amethyst

angelite

aquamarine

blue lace agate

fluorite

howlite

jade

lepidolite

rose quartz

selenite

POWER

amethyst

black opal

black tourmaline

carnelian

citrine

clear quartz

garnet

lapis lazuli

Lemurian seed

onyx

pyrite

red jasper

ruby

sunstone

tiger's eye

topaz

PROPHETIC DREAMS

amethyst

clear quartz

dream quartz

Herkimer diamond

labradorite

lapis lazuli

moldavite

moonstone

prehnite

sodalite

PROSPERITY

carnelian

citrine

goldstone

green aventurine

green jade

malachite

moss agate

peridot

pyrite

ruby

tiger's eye

topaz

PROTECTION

amber

amethyst

Apache tears

black tourmaline

green aventurine

hematite

jade

labradorite

lapis lazuli

lepidolite
mookaite jasper
obsidian
selenite
smoky quartz
tiger's eye

PSYCHIC POWERS

amethyst
apophyllite
aquamarine
azurite
blue or green kyanite
clear quartz
fluorite
labradorite
lapis lazuli
larimar
moldavite
moonstone
selenite
sodalite

PURIFICATION

amethyst
Apache tears
black tourmaline
calcite
chlorite quartz
citrine

clear quartz
flint
fluorite
halite
hematite
obsidian
rose quartz
selenite
smoky quartz

SLEEP

amethyst
angelite
fluorite
howlite
lepidolite
moonstone
rose quartz
selenite
sodalite
smoky quartz

SPIRITS—TO CALL

amethyst
angelite
apophyllite
black obsidian
clear quartz
labradorite
lapis lazuli

moldavite

moonstone

selenite

SPIRITUALITY

amethyst

aurora quartz

black tourmaline

Celtic quartz

clear quartz

golden healer

labradorite

lapis lazuli

Lemurian seed

moldavite

moonstone

petalite

selenite

trigoniz quartz

STRENGTH

black tourmaline

bloodstone

carnelian

garnet

onyx

red jasper

tiger's eyet

SUCCESS

citrine

green aventurine

jade

malachite

pyrite

ruby

tiger's eye

VISIONS

amethyst

azurite

iolite

labradorite

lapis lazuli

moldavite

moonstone

WISDOM

amethyst

clear quartz

fluorite

lapis lazuli

sapphire

sodalite

tiger's eye

WISHES

aurora quartz

Celtic quartz

citrine

clear quartz

green aventurine

Lemurian seed

moldavite

moonstone

petalite

pyrite

rose quartz

selenite

tiger's eye

trigoniz quartz

YOUTH—TO MAINTAIN

amethyst

clear quartz

aventurine

citrine

jade

rose quartz

turquoise

Appendix C
Herbs by Elemental and Energetic Attribute

The four elements—Earth, Air, Fire, Water—are traditionally associated with either feminine or masculine energy. These designations go back thousands of years. When working with these energies it's important to keep in mind that "masculine" and "feminine" are not the same as "male" and "female." These energetic designations have nothing to do with gender or sexual identity. In other traditions, these complementing energies are labeled in many other ways, such as yin/yang, above/below, action/intuition, and so forth. When working with herbs for elemental magick, you are working with these masculine and feminine energetic qualities—these are not herbs for males or herbs for females.

EARTH

Feminine energy. These herbs are best used in magicks for:

MONEY. PROSPERITY. FERTILITY. HEALING. EMPLOYMENT. PROTECTION. NATURE. GROUNDING. STRENGTH. SUCCESS. STABILITY. WISDOM. DEATH. REBIRTH. TRUTH. ABUNDANCE.

barley	oats
buckwheat	sorrel
honeysuckle	vervain
horehound	vetiver
mugwort	

AIR

Masculine energy. These herbs are best used in magicks for:

MENTAL POWERS. VISIONS. PSYCHIC POWERS. WISDOM. ASTRAL
PROJECTION. THOUGHTS. CLARITY. KNOWLEDGE. DIVINATION. MEMORY.
SHADOW WORK. VISUALIZATION. CREATIVITY. NEW BEGINNINGS.
PURIFICATION. INSPIRATION.

acacia	dandelion	mint
agrimony	elecampane	palm, date
almond	fenugreek	parsley
anise	goldenrod	pecan
bergamot, orange	hazelnut	pine
borage	lavender	pistachio
Brazil nut	lemongrass	rice
caraway	lemon verbena	sage
chicory	linden	savory, summer
citron	maple	star anise
clover	marjoram	

FIRE

Masculine energy. These herbs are best used in magicks for:

LUST. COURAGE. STRENGTH. EXORCISM. PROTECTION. HEALTH.
PURIFICATION. HEALING. ENERGY. DESTRUCTION. POWER.
WILLPOWER. SEXUALITY. PASSION. TRANSFORMATION.

allspice	bay	cashew
angelica	calendula	celery
basil	carrot	chestnut

chili pepper

chrysanthemum

cinnamon

cinquefoil

clove

cumin

damiana

dill

fennel

fig

galangal

garlic

ginger

ginseng

hawthorn

hyssop

lime

marigold

mullein

mustard

nettle

nutmeg

olive

onion

orange

pepper

peppermint

pineapple

pomegranate

rooibos

rosemary

saffron

tangerine

tea

thistle, milk

tormentil

walnut

woodruff

wormwood

yerba maté

WATER

Feminine energy. These herbs are best used in magicks for:
SLEEP. MEDITATION. PURIFICATION. PROPHETIC DREAMS. HEALING.
LOVE. FRIENDSHIPS. FIDELITY. ILLUSIONS. ENCHANTMENTS.
DIVINATION. DREAMS. EMOTIONS. INTUITION. LUNAR MAGICK.
REFLECTION. PEACE.

apple

apricot

aster

bachelor's button

balm, lemon

banana

blackberry

cardamom

catnip

chamomile

cherry

chickweed

coconut

cucumber

elder

feverfew

geranium

grape

hemp

hibiscus

jasmine

lemon

licorice

lilac

lily

mallow

papaya

passionflower

peach

pear

plum

raspberry

rose

skullcap

spearmint

strawberry

sugarcane

thyme

valerian

vanilla

violet

willow

yarrow

Appendix D
Herb Substitutions

Depending on your geographic location and the time of year, you may find that certain herbs are not available in your area. If necessary, the following substitutions are recommended.

GENERAL

Rose petals may substitute any flower

Cinnamon may substitute any spice

Rosemary may substitute any herb

Lemon may substitute any fruit

Dandelion may substitute any root or toxic plant

Bergamot—Half Lemon Peel/Half Orange Peel

Chamomile—Jasmine

Cinnamon—Nutmeg, or any spice

Clove—Nutmeg

Ginger—Cinnamon

Hemp—Bay

Hyssop—Lavender

Jasmine—Rose Petals

Juniper Berries—Pine

Lavender—Rose Petals

Lemon—May substitute any fruits

Lemongrass—Lemon Peel

Lemon Peel—Lemongrass

Lemon Verbena—Lemongrass

Marigolds—Rose Petals

Mint—Sage

Mugwort—Dandelion Leaf

Nutmeg—Cinnamon

Orange Peel—Tangerine Peel

Peppermint—Spearmint

Pine—Juniper Berries

Rose—Yarrow

Rosemary—Thyme, or any herb

Saffron—Orange Peel

Sage—Mints

Spearmint—Peppermint

Tea—Rooibos

Thyme—Rosemary

Vanilla—Woodruff

Woodruff—Vanilla Bean

Wormwood—Dandelion Leaf

Yarrow—Rose Petals

Appendix E
Latin Names of Herbs

ACACIA—*Acacia senegal*

AGRIMONY—*Agrimonia eupatoria*

ALFALFA—*Medicago sativa*

ALLSPICE—*Pimenta officinalis or P. dioica*

ALMOND—*Prunus dulcis*

ANGELICA—*Angelica archangelica*

ANISE—*Pimpinella anisum*

APPLE—*Pyrus* spp.

APRICOT—*Prunus armeniaca*

ASTER—*Callistephus chinensis*

BACHELOR'S BUTTON—*Centaurea cyanus*

BALM, LEMON—*Melissa officinalis*

BANANA—*Musa sapientum*

BARLEY—*Hordeum vulgare*

BASIL—*Ocimum basilicum*

BAY—*Laurus nobilis*

BERGAMOT, ORANGE—*Mentha citrata*

BLACKBERRY—*Rubus villosus*

BLUEBERRY—*Vaccinium sect. Cyanococcus*

BORAGE—*Borago officinalis*

BRAZIL NUT—*Bertholletia excelsa*

BUCKWHEAT—*Fagopyrum* spp.

CARAWAY—*Carum carvi*

CARDAMOM—*Elettaria cardamomum*

CARNATION—*Dianthus caryophyllus*

CARROT—*Daucus carota*

CASHEW—*Anacardium occidentale*

CATNIP—*Nepeta cataria*

CELERY—*Apium graveolens*

CHAMOMILE, ROMAN— *Chamaemelum nobile*

CHERRY—*Prunus avium*

CHESTNUT—*Castanea sativa*

CHICKWEED—*Stellaria media*

CHICORY—*Cichorium intybus*

CHILI PEPPER—*Capsicum* spp.

CHRYSANTHEMUM— *Chrysanthemum*

CINNAMON—*Cinnamomum verum*

CINQUEFOIL—*Potentilla*

CITRON—*Citrus medica*

CLOVE—*Syzygium aromaticum*

CLOVER—*Trifolium* spp.

COCONUT—*Cocos nucifera*

COHOSH, BLACK—*Cimicifuga racemosa*

CORIANDER—*Coriandrum sativum*

CUCUMBER—*Cucumis sativus*

CUMIN—*Cuminum cyinum*

DAMIANA—*Turnera diffusa*

DANDELION—*Taraxacum officinale*

DILL—*Anethum graveolens*

ECHINACEA—*Echinacea angustifolia*

ELDER, AMERICAN—*Sambucus canadensis*

ELECAMPANE—*Inula helenium*

FENNEL—*Foeniculum vulgare*

FENUGREEK—*Trigonella foenum-graecum*

FEVERFEW—*Tanacetum parthenium*

FIG—*Ficus carica*

GALANGAL—*Alpinia galanga*

GARLIC—*Allium sativum*

GERANIUM—*Pelargonium*

GINGER—*Zingiber officinale*

GINSENG, AMERICAN—*Panax quinquefolius*

GOLDENROD—*Solidago*

GRAPE—*Vitis vinifera*

HAWTHORN—*Crataegus oxyacantha*

HAZELNUT, AMERICAN—*Corylus americana*

HEMP—*Cannabis sativa*

HIBISCUS—*Hibiscus* spp.

HONEYSUCKLE—*Lonicera*

HOPS—*Humulus lupulus*

HYSSOP—*Hyssopus officinalis*

JASMINE—*Jasminum officinale*

LAVENDER—*Lavandula officinalis*

LEMON—*Citrus limon*

LEMONGRASS—*Cymbopogon citratus*

LEMON VERBENA—*Lippia citriodora*

LETTUCE—*Lactuca sativa*

LICORICE—*Glycyrrhiza glabra*

LILAC—*Syringa vulgaris*

LILY—*Lilium brownii*

LIME—*Citrus x aurantiifolia*

LINDEN—*Tilia x europaea*

MALLOW—*Malva sylvestris*

MAPLE—*Acer* spp.

MARIGOLD—*Calendula officinalis*

MARJORAM—*Origanum majorana*

MINT—*Mentha* spp.

MUGWORT—*Artemisia vulgaris*

MULLEIN—*Verbascum thapsus*

MUSTARD SEED—*Sinapis alba*

NETTLE—*Urtica dioica*

NUTMEG—*Myristica fragrans*

OAT—*Avena sativa*

OLIVE—*Olea europaea*

ONION—*Allium cepa*

ORANGE—*Citrus sinensis*

PALM, DATE—*Phoenix dactylifera*

PANSY—*Viola tricolor*

PAPAYA—*Carica papaya*

PARSLEY—*Petroselinum crispum*

PASSIONFLOWER—*Passiflora incarnata*

PEACH—*Prunus persica*

PEAR—*Pyrus communis*

PECAN—*Carya illinoinensis*

PEPPER—*Piper nigrum*

PEPPERMINT—*Mentha piperita*

PINE—*Pinus spp.*

PINEAPPLE—*Ananas comosus*

PISTACHIO—*Pistacia vera*

PLUM—*Prunus domestica*

POMEGRANATE—*Punica granatum*

POTATO—*Solanium tuberosum*

RASPBERRY—*Rubus idaeus*

RICE—*Oryza sativa*

ROOIBOS—*Aspalathus linearis*

ROSE—*Rosa* spp.

ROSEMARY—*Rosmarinus officinalis*

SAFFRON—*Crocus sativus*

SAGE—*Salvia officinalis*

SAVORY, SUMMER—*Satureja hortensis*

SKULLCAP, BLUE—*Scutellaria lateriflora*

SORREL—*Rumex acetosa*

SPEARMINT—*Mentha spicata*

STAR ANISE—*Illicium verum*

STRAWBERRY—*Fragaria vesca*

SUGARCANE—*Saccharum officinarum*

TEA—*Camellia sinensis*

THISTLE, MILK—*Silybum marianum*

THYME—*Thymus vulgaris*

TORMENTIL—*Potentilla erecta*

TURMERIC—*Curcuma longa*

VALERIAN—*Valeriana officinalis*

VANILLA—*Vanilla aromatica*

VERVAIN—*Verbena officinalis*

VETIVER—*Chrysopogon zizanioides*

VIOLET—*Viola odorata*

WALNUT—*Juglans regia*

WILLOW—*Salix alba*

WOODRUFF—*Asperula odorata*

WORMWOOD—*Artemisia absinthium*

YARROW—*Achillea millefolium*

YERBA MATÉ—*Ilex paraguariensis*

Resources

BOOKS

Adams Media. *The Encyclopedia of Crystals, Herbs, and New Age Elements: An A to Z Guide to New Age Elements and How to Use Them.* New York: Adams Media, 2016.

Baker, Margaret. *Gardener's Magic and Folklore.* New York: Universe Books, a division of Rizzoli International Publications, 1978.

Blackwell, Will H. *Poisonous and Medicinal Plants.* Hoboken, NJ: Prentice Hall, 1989).

Blunt, Wilfrid, and Sandra Raphael. *The Ilustrated Herbal.* London: Frances Lincoln, Ltd., a division of Quarto Group, 1979.

Boland, Bridget. *Gardener's Magic and Other Old Wives' Lore.* London: Michael Omara Books, 2003.

Chevallier, Andrew. *Encyclopedia of Herbal Medicine: 550 Herbs and Remedies for Common Ailments.* London: DK, a division of Penguin Books, 2016.

Cunningham, Scott. *Cunningham's Encyclopedia of Crystal, Gem & Metal Magic.* Woodbury, MN: Llewellyn Publications, 1998.

———. *Cunningham's Encyclopedia of Magical Herbs.* St. Paul, MN: Llewellyn Publications, 1985.

———. *Divination for Beginners: Reading the Past, Present & Future.* Woodbury, MN: Llewellyn Publications, 2003.

Desantis, Lawrence, CHC, ND. *Herbology.* Algonquin, IL: New Eden School of Natural Health & Herbal Studies, n.d.

———. *Natural Health and Nutrition.* Algonquin, IL: New Eden School of Natural Health & Herbal Studies, n.d..

Frazier, Karen. *An Introduction to Crystal Grids: Daily Rituals for Your Heart, Health, and Happiness.* Berkeley, CA: Rockridge Press, 2020.

Hall, Judy. *The Crystal Bible.* Iola, WI: Krause Publications, 2003.

———. *The Ultimate Guide to Crystal Grids: Transform Your Life Using the Power of Crystals and Layouts.* Beverly, MA: Fair Winds Press, 2017.

Harlow, S. M. *A Tea Witch's Grimoire: Magickal Recipes for Your Tea Time.* Newburyport, MA: Weiser Books, 2023.

Jacob, Dorothy. *A Witch's Guide to Gardening.* Taplinger Publishing Company, 1965 (no longer in business).

Johnston, Sarah Iles. *Ancient Greek Divination.* New York: John Wiley, 2008.

Mégemont, Florence. *The Metaphysical Book of Gems and Crystals.* Rochester, VT: Healing Arts Press, an imprint of Inner Traditions, 2007.

WEBSITES

GemSociety.org—A database with scientific and technical information about crystals

Index of Spells, Recipes, and Rituals

About the Author

S. M. Harlow is a passionate tea connoisseur, master herbalist, and a seeker of holistic wellness. With a profound devotion to the transformative power of botanicals, Susana has seamlessly woven her deep knowledge of tea into the fabric of spiritual and physical healing. Her first book, the bestselling *A Tea Witch's Grimoire*, has become an essential guide for those seeking to explore the mystical synergy between herbal infusions and wellness, offering readers a unique perspective on brewing rituals that harmonize body, mind, and spirit.

Beyond her expertise in the world of tea, Susana is a certified crystal healer and Reiki master, as she continues to pursue her education toward becoming a doctor of traditional naturopathy. Susana also proficiently practices in different arts of divination, including tea-leaf readings, palmistry, tarot, and oracles, further deepening her connection with those she guides, offering insights and foresight through this ancient art.

When she is not writing, hosting tea ceremonies, and studying, Susana devotes her time to her husband and son on their homestead in Alabama.

To Our Readers

Weiser Books, an imprint of Red Wheel/Weiser, publishes books across the entire spectrum of occult, esoteric, speculative, and New Age subjects. Our mission is to publish quality books that will make a difference in people's lives without advocating any one particular path or field of study. We value the integrity, originality, and depth of knowledge of our authors.

Our readers are our most important resource, and we appreciate your input, suggestions, and ideas about what you would like to see published.

Visit our website at www.redwheelweiser.com, where you can learn about our upcoming books and free downloads, and also find links to sign up for our newsletter and exclusive offers.

You can also contact us at info@rwwbooks.com or at

Red Wheel/Weiser, LLC
65 Parker Street, Suite 7
Newburyport, MA 01950